A Journey into

Matisse's

Sou...

Laura McPhee

ArtPlace Series

Roaring Forties Press
Berkeley, California

Roaring Forties Press
1053 Santa Fe Avenue
Berkeley, California 94706

ISBN 0-9766706-9-0

Library of Congress Cataloging-in-Publication Data
McPhee, Laura.
    A Journey into Matisse's South of France / Laura McPhee.
    p. cm.—(ArtPlace series)
        Includes bibliographical references and index.
        ISBN 0-9766706-9-0 (alk. paper)
    1. Matisse, Henri, 1869-1954—Homes and haunts—France, Southern.
    2. Artists—France—Biography. 3. France, Southern—Description and travel.
    I. Title. II. Series.
    N6853.M33M47 2006
    759.4—dc2

                                                                    2006014118

For Aaron Barsky: "To Sir, With Love"

Contents

Acknowledgments

There are a lot of people to whom I owe a tremendous amount for helping me complete this book. First and foremost, a huge thanks to Deirdre Greene and Roaring Forties Press for giving me such a great opportunity and for being so supportive. And I would be woefully remiss if I did not acknowledge how invaluable the recent work of Hilary Spurling has been to this project. Her two-volume biography of Henri Matisse is the most comprehensive and accurate account of the artist, and I could never have filled in so many gaps without her books as a primary research tool. I also could not have written this book without the love and support of so many family members and friends—Missy, Miriam, Rosalie, Susan, Rod, Debra, and Sean—you bring out the best in me! Thank you to my parents, Judy and Steve, for continuing to believe in me. A big thank you to Ian and Samantha for putting up with a mom who keeps a crazy schedule and a not-so-tidy house. I love you very, very much. Thanks most of all to Kevin McKinney, Jim Poyser, and everyone at *NUVO* for allowing me to chase my dreams around the world and still come home to you. I really am the luckiest girl in the world.

A Journey into
Matisse's
South of France

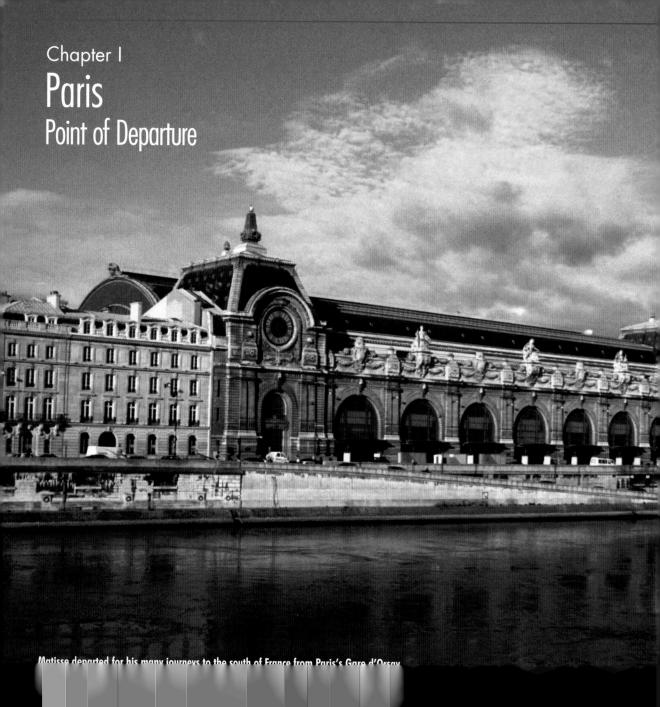

Chapter I
Paris
Point of Departure

Matisse departed for his many journeys to the south of France from Paris's Gare d'Orsay

Henri Matisse came to his craft relatively late in life, having reached the age of twenty-one before he began his formal training and thirty-five before he saw his first true success. Because of his late start, Matisse was loath to waste time or stagnate. He became an artist constantly on the move, figuratively and literally, as soon as he identified his path.

Although Matisse has been canonized as one of the first great painters of the twentieth century, the perpetual evolution of his style has led some to criticize his work as inconsistent or even incoherent. In truth, Matisse did not belong exclusively to any nineteenth- or twentieth-century artistic movement. He was at various times an Impressionist, a Pointillist, an Expressionist, a Cubist, and most famously a Fauve; he was as renowned for his portraits and landscapes as he was for his still lifes and nude studies.

Much of this variety came from his frequent journeys to the south of France. Matisse was never a stay-at-home artist. He believed that traveling to new places was a way for a painter to cleanse the visual palette and that seeing an unfamiliar world in an unfamiliar light would help him gain a fresh vision. Each of his journeys to strange and new locations pushed him further toward the freedom of expression he sought to achieve on canvas. "The search for color did not come to me from studying paintings," Matisse explained, "but from the outside—that is, from the revelation of light in nature."

Born in a small northern village near the Belgian border, Henri Matisse spent his entire life moving southward toward color and light. For more than fifty years, the dogged pursuit of color led him to some of the most remote villages in the south of France, as well as to some of its most popular locations. In towns such as St. Tropez, Collioure, Nice, Vence, and Cimiez, he found both refuge and courage to push his painting forward. The pure color of the teal skies, emerald hills, red soil, and indigo seas of the Mediterranean were so powerful that Matisse often wore dark glasses while painting because he feared he might go blind by spending so many hours reproducing those intense colors on his canvases.

The Boy from Bohain

Henri Matisse was not the first member of his family to go to Paris to seek his fortune. In the years before the birth of their first child, his young parents left their small northern village to work in the capital. Anna found employment in a hat shop, and Henri Sr. bought fabrics for a large fashion house. The couple returned north for the holidays to stay with Henri's parents in the small village of Le Cateau-Cambrésis, a town the Matisse family had lived in for centuries. Henri-Emile-Benoît Matisse was born at 8 p.m. on December 31, 1869, in his grandfather's two-room weaver's cottage.

Matisse was eight days old when his parents moved him the nineteen miles to

Bohain-en-Vermandois, where Henri Sr. had purchased a general store selling everything from seeds to silk. Over the next two decades, Matisse's father streamlined the enterprise into a wholesale and resale company with a thriving business in town and a fleet of wagons delivering seed and fertilizer to the many turnip farms throughout the flat, dark, and wet Picardy region.

Despite his father's agrarian business, Matisse spent his childhood in town, under the dour and gray northern skies, in a treeless and polluted landscape. The last remnants of Bohain's great forest had been cut down the year before Henri's birth, and he grew up surrounded by smoking factory chimneys in a countryside constantly shrinking as a result of convulsive industrialization. The store and the family's first home, which was rented apartments above the business, were located on the newly built main thoroughfare, Rue du Château.

21 BOHAIN — Rue du Château

Druon, édit., Bohain

The Matisse family lived on this street in Bohain in an apartment above the family store beginning in 1870. Within a few years, Henri Sr. was able to buy a house for the family on the outskirts of town.

Many of the factories that flourished in northern France at the turn of the twentieth century now stand abandoned.

Henri Matisse with his mother, Anna, just before Matisse left to study law in Paris in 1887.

The majority of the town's eight thousand residents worked at one of its forty-two factories, all but a handful of which produced luxury fabrics destined for Paris. The weavers of Bohain were renowned for their skill, the richness of their colors, and the daring of their designs.

Despite the beauty of the town's textiles, however, there was little encouragement for creative pursuits in the sternly utilitarian and increasingly industrial society of Matisse's youth. Bohain had no museum or art gallery. There were no paintings to speak of in the town hall or church, and certainly none in the modest homes of the merchants and factory workers.

By the age of eighteen, Matisse felt increasing pressure to take over the family store, a prospect he saw as both his duty and his doom. Unwilling to do so just yet, Henri proposed a compromise. He asked to spend a year in Paris studying for the law exam. His father agreed, and though he had no real interest in law or any other career, Matisse got out of Bohain and out of the seed business.

The year he spent studying law in Paris had little impact on the young Matisse. By his own admission, he was so disinterested in art that he never even visited the Louvre. Unimpressed and uninspired, Matisse returned home in 1888 and found a job as a copyist of legal briefs. It was mind-numbing work. Every case required dozens of documents dozens of pages long, all of which had to be copied by hand. A decade before the first primitive commercial fountain pens were available, Matisse was copying the legal documents with goose-feather quills, using sand as a blotter.

He was miserable. And within the year he was hospitalized. Although his illness would now be recognized as a hernia, most likely caused by a youth spent loading bags of seeds onto his father's wagons, throughout his life Matisse considered it a physical manifestation of his anxiety about his future.

While in the hospital recuperating, he shared a room with a local textile worker's son whose hobby was copying paintings in oils from reproductions. Matisse decided to try the same distraction. His mother purchased him a small kit of "chromos," with profound results: "From the moment I held the box of colors in my hand," said Matisse, "I knew this was my life."

He bought a "do-it-yourself" painting manual and studied it for months while regaining his health, producing small landscape and still-life replicas. As soon as he returned to work as a law clerk, he began taking art classes every morning and evening, sometimes squeezing another in during his lunch break. His natural abilities were obvious to the other students and his instructors, and he quickly advanced through the available classes. Before long, Matisse had devised yet another plan for getting out of Bohain.

In 1891, he asked his father for permission to return to Paris to study for a teaching diploma in art. By this time, Matisse was already known as a bit of a disappointment in his hometown. His frail health, failure to take over his father's business, unambitious law career, and now his desire to be a painter cemented his reputation as the town fool: *le sot Matisse*.

It would be hard to exaggerate the small community's shock over Matisse's career plan. To many, it was quite simply a disgrace. "There were no painters in my family; there was no painter in my region," said Matisse. He was the first, and for a long time the only, painter Bohain produced. And his family was appalled.

Although he had been to Paris as a law student a few years earlier, twenty-one-year-old Henri Matisse made the first of his many artistic journeys south when he left home for Paris in October 1891. It would be a long time before he returned to Bohain, longer still before he returned a success. But Matisse never looked back. "Before, nothing interested me," he said about his departure from his hometown. "Afterwards, I had nothing in my head but painting."

Center of the Artistic Universe

Henri Matisse's decision to move to Paris and become a painter in 1891 meant a long and elaborate education at a time when both the nature and the function of painting were being redefined. At the end of the nineteenth century, artistic values—indeed, values of all kind—were being called into question, and Paris was the epicenter of the controversy.

For decades French academicism had been the standard by which Western art was judged, and only artists from the Beaux-Arts tradition, particularly graduates of the prestigious Ecole des Beaux-Arts in Paris, stood any real chance of success. Academic art had the support of the critics, the public, and the government. A broad public sanction, backed by rich patronage, encouraged the development of an official art that was accepted as "good art." Painters from around the world were coming to Paris in larger numbers than ever before—all vying for entrance into the prestigious French art system. According to the French government, the number of artists living in Paris doubled between 1870 and 1914, giving it the distinction of having more artists than any other city in the world.

The French tradition had been weakened substantially by the brash originality of Impressionism a few years earlier, and there was a resurgence of devotion to the "old school" ways in the face of the strange new style of paintings that Postimpressionist artists such as Cézanne, Gauguin, and van Gogh were beginning to produce with growing success. Branded as rebels for their desire to discover "the future of painting, not suffocate in the past," this new generation of artists was soon known as the Indépendants, and though they were slowly gaining recognition and success when Matisse arrived in Paris, "good society" still viewed the interlopers with suspicion and ridicule.

Rather than feeling hopeful about his newfound passion and the pursuit of his dream, Matisse felt despair at being left behind, a growing fear that he could never compensate for his lack of early training. "I was like

someone who'd arrived in a country where they speak a different language," he said. "I couldn't melt into the crowd; I couldn't fall into step with the rest."

Matisse was older, less experienced, and without the needed credentials to enter ❶ the Ecole des Beaux-Arts, 14 rue Bonaparte, through the front door when he reached Paris at the start of fall term in October 1891, and like the majority of those seeking admission, he failed to pass the entrance exam. He and the others denied admission enrolled in various private academies and began taking classes taught by former and current Beaux-Arts faculty in preparation for the next round of tests.

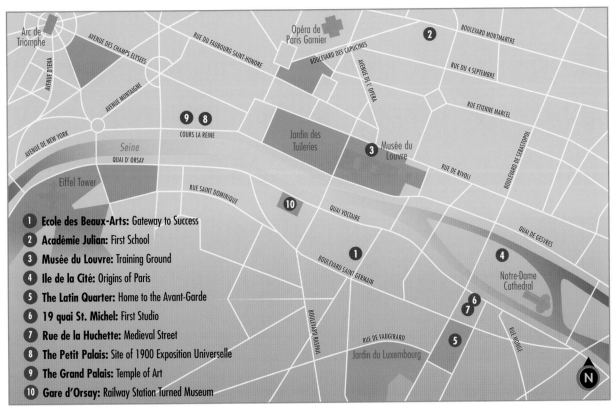

❶ **Ecole des Beaux-Arts:** Gateway to Success
❷ **Académie Julian:** First School
❸ **Musée du Louvre:** Training Ground
❹ **Ile de la Cité:** Origins of Paris
❺ **The Latin Quarter:** Home to the Avant-Garde
❻ **19 quai St. Michel:** First Studio
❼ **Rue de la Huchette:** Medieval Street
❽ **The Petit Palais:** Site of 1900 Exposition Universelle
❾ **The Grand Palais:** Temple of Art
❿ **Gare d'Orsay:** Railway Station Turned Museum

Gustave Moreau

Moreau was a classically trained academic artist whose intense, allegorical works were often inspired by what he claimed were supernatural visions. His large-scale and elaborate compositions often feature a mythological female subject in a dreamlike landscape. This dream state, however, is not a representation of the Freudian subconscious, as in later works by the Surrealists; rather, it is triggered by sensual experience and represents an escape from the struggles of the quotidian. Moreau and his Beaux-Arts contemporaries focused on luxurious beauty and sensuality as symbolic representations of perfection and harmony—the same aesthetic that would later come to define the Belle Epoque.

Matisse switched schools after one frustrating term at the prestigious ❷ Académie Julian, located near the Paris Opera in the Passage des Panoramas, 11 boulevard Montmartre, and began studying with Gustave Moreau, who himself had come through the Beaux-Arts system as a young painter and was now a senior faculty member. Moreau believed that the best training for aspiring painters was to avoid the frivolity of Impressionism and concentrate instead on copying the masterpieces of French art found in the Louvre.

Matisse (seated) with fellow students at the Académie Julian, 1891.

Hesiod and the Muse contains all the quintessential elements of Gustave Moreau's work. Here, the mythological female muse drapes her arms around the Greek writer Hesiod in a lush ideological background, evoking the sensuality and the mysticism for which Moreau was known.

Three years and four failed attempts later, Matisse was finally granted admission to the Ecole des Beaux-Arts, thanks in large part to the influence of his teacher, Moreau. Although he still had to depend on an allowance from his father to cover his monthly living expenses, being a student at the official academy provided Matisse with a certain amount of status, as well as access to studios, a variety of instructors, the school's vast library and private collections, and the chance to compete for worthwhile prizes.

The years Matisse spent at the Ecole des Beaux-Arts provided innumerable benefits. He had stimulating peers, gained official recognition as an artist, and even sold a few of his reproductions, one of which hung in the country residence of the French head of state.

Musée du Louvre

In the early 1890s, Matisse worked methodically through the encyclopedia of Western art in the ❸ Musée du Louvre, 99 rue de Rivoli. Although he believed that art could and should boldly pursue new expressions, Matisse also revered the masters who preceded him, and he knew that a grounding in the classics was a necessary part of his education, including meticulous reproductions of great works by those he admired.

The origin of the Louvre's collection can be traced to François I, who purchased a number of Italian paintings for the royal collection, including Leonardo da Vinci's *Mona Lisa*. During Louis XIV's reign, the collection numbered a mere two hundred works, but donations accepted in lieu of bad debts helped it grow exponentially.

The museum first opened to the public in 1793, not long after the French Revolution. The first exhibition was held alongside the annual Beaux-Arts Salon and contained more than five hundred paintings and objects from former royal collections. Directors of the

Additionally, he was beginning to lay the groundwork for his artistic independence.

The First of Many Offenses

In 1897, Matisse decided to take a risk by submitting his painting *The Dining Table* for the annual student exhibition, the Salon de la Société Nationale des Beaux-Arts. Impressionism was still considered somewhat scandalous, certainly beyond the boundaries of good taste, and this painting came so close to Impressionism that even Matisse's friends worried that he had gone mad by submitting such a daring work for exhibition. His girlfriend of five years, Camille, begged

The Louvre, the residence of French kings until the 1670s.

museum welcomed the people into the palace that now belonged to the nation to view the masterpieces of art history that now belonged to them.

him not to jeopardize his career and their future by showing the painting publicly.

The Salon de la Société Nationale des Beaux-Arts opened on April 27, 1897. Matisse showed *The Dining Table* along with four small still lifes. Although he had been praised at the student exhibition the year before, with one critic calling his still life "among the best things at the salon," Beaux-Arts authorities were outraged by *The Dining Table*. They accused Matisse of trying to capitalize on the sensationalism of the Impressionists to garner attention for himself. Despite his distaste for Impressionism, Moreau stood by his student and praised the realistic details of the painting, commenting to a group of spectators that the decanters on the table were so well done he could hang his hat on them.

Matisse's father came to Paris for the opening, but shook his head and lamented his inability to understand the paintings he saw in his son's studio. He stood at the exhibit and listened as people stopped to comment on how shocking and horrible his son's painting was. For the rest of his life, Matisse would talk in great detail and with visible sadness about how his father saw only his numerous failures and how he regretted being such a disappointment to the man whose approval he never received.

Matisse had gambled and lost with *The Dining Table*. At the time, he thought he'd lost everything. He gave himself one more year in Paris and decided he would live that last year on his own terms. "In effect, I was going to be forced to take another profession," he explained. "So I decided to take a year off, avoid all hindrances, and paint the way I wanted. I worked only for myself."

Although *The Dining Table* (1897) depicts an everyday scene, a maid leaning over a table to make final adjustments to a floral centerpiece on an elaborately set table, the painting has hints of the Matisse about to emerge. The perspective of the painting is askew, much as in Degas's Impressionist work, and the colors are occasionally a little too bright for such a delicate scene. The pure color of the fruit, the starkness of the white tablecloth, and the overall absence of tone hint at the boldness Matisse would become famous for a decade later. The painting may look innocuous to twenty-first-century viewers, but these small elements were so daring that they were considered scandalous at the time.

Paris Muse: Camille

Caroline Joblaud was nineteen years old when she met Henri Matisse in the summer of 1892. An orphan from the provinces, she had never worn a store-bought dress or a lady's slippers until she arrived in Paris and found work as a shopgirl in one of the large new department stores. To suit her new identity, country girl Caroline reinvented herself and changed her name to Camille.

Caroline Joblaud (Camille), 1893–94.

The Reader (1895) features Camille as the model and was first exhibited at the Salon de la Société Nationale des Beaux-Arts in 1896.

The couple split in 1897, and when Matisse married Amélie Parayre the next year, Marguerite came to live with them and was raised as their daughter. Camille eventually moved to Brittany, where she married a schoolmaster many years later. Although she and Matisse didn't communicate directly after their breakup, Marguerite often visited her birth mother, bringing news of one to the other,

Keeping up a stylish appearance in Paris was expensive, so Camille worked as an artist's model to earn extra money. She met Matisse while posing for a fellow student at Moreau's studio. Within a few months of their meeting, Camille and Matisse set up house in a tiny Left Bank apartment overlooking the Seine. Social values of the time prevented Matisse's parents from accepting the relationship, particularly when their son's mistress became pregnant.

On August 31, 1894, Henri and Camille became the parents of Marguerite Emilienne Matisse. Henri Sr. couldn't bring himself to cut off his son's allowance completely, leaving the young family with no income, but Matisse's father did have a legal document drawn up the day before the birth of his first granddaughter, blocking the automatic right of his son's heir to any of his estate.

and Matisse sent Camille money until the end of his life. Matisse seldom spoke of his relationship with his "first wife," though he remarked as he neared his eightieth birthday that he hadn't needed imagination at twenty-five to know how it felt to be in love.

The earliest surviving sculptures by Matisse are a pair of terra-cotta medallions bearing bas-relief portraits of Camille's head, and paintings with her as his model were among the first he exhibited. More than fifty years after their student days in Paris, Leon Vassaux came to visit Matisse at La Rêve in Vence. Vassaux brought with him one of the clay medallions of Camille, and Matisse began incorporating the medallion as a decorative element in his last paintings, all done in Vence in 1947. In a series of still lifes, Matisse ended his career with the face of the woman who was there at its beginning.

Left Bank Atelier

The history of Paris dates back more than two thousand years. In 55 B.C., the Romans conquered a small fishing village on a tiny island in the middle of the Seine inhabited by the Parisii tribe and established a settlement on what became known as ❹ Ile de la Cité that quickly spilled over the river and onto its left bank.

Since the Middle Ages, the Left Bank of Paris has been synonymous with the city's artistic and intellectual communities. Growing out of the neighborhoods surrounding the Sorbonne, this area between Notre-Dame Cathedral and Luxembourg Gardens became known as ❺ the Latin Quarter, so named because Latin was the required lingua franca of university students until the mid-eighteenth century.

Matisse changed residences five times in his first precarious hand-to-mouth year in Paris before renting his first studio in the Latin Quarter—a windowless attic, little more than a cupboard lit by a skylight over the bed, on the sixth floor at ❻ 19 quai St. Michel.

At the time, the Left Bank was plagued by abject poverty, rampant disease, overcrowding, lack of sewers, and a shantytown building mentality. Much of the area around Notre-Dame, including the building Matisse called home, came to be declared an *îlot insalubre*—an

The exterior of 19 quai St. Michel underwent extensive renovation in the 1980s, but much of the interior remains unchanged since Matisse first rented a studio here in 1892.

The winding cobblestone streets of the Latin Quarter behind quai St. Michel have been home to small cafés and unique shopping for centuries. During Matisse's struggling student days, he often lived on less than the equivalent of twenty-five cents a day, including a cheap meal of bread and broth at a café located behind his building.

urban housing block considered a public health risk due to its high rates of tuberculosis and infant mortality. In the words of one government official, the entire area was little more than "a cauldron of . . . poverty, disease, delinquency, and crime."

Henri Matisse and Amélie Parayre around the time of their wedding in January 1898.

The massive stone building at 19 quai St. Michel was more than a hundred years old when Matisse first took up residence in 1892, and it had already been divided and redivided so many times that it resembled a vertical village. Twisted staircases split off or doubled back to the streets below and also led to landings with doors that opened into bookstores, cafés, secondhand furniture shops, artists' studios, or family apartments. The narrow ❼ Rue de la Huchette, behind the building, continues to be lined with small cafés and family-run businesses; the main entrance to 19 quai St. Michel faces the Seine.

Partially hidden between postcard turnstiles and the dark blue awnings of the Pub Saint Michel, two massive green doors mark the entrance, as does the obligatory blue-and-white Parisian address tile. The facade was renovated in the 1980s, but much of the building's structure remains unchanged. Beyond the glass security door, wooden stairs lead up from the small lobby to a second-floor mezzanine. Apartments line the street side of the building, and two staircases lead up from either end of the wide mezzanine. Three more floors of landings and doors create a maze of passages in the quiet, dark building. A century later, one hundred and two steps still lead to the original door of Matisse's studio.

Rebounding from his artistic failure and the breakup with Camille the summer before, Matisse married twenty-five-year-old Amélie Parayre in January 1898. The young couple had met at the wedding of mutual friends three months earlier, and both claimed an immediate attraction. Amélie was from a relatively affluent Toulouse family, and though he always considered her and the women in her family "Spanish queens," Matisse was as honest about his intentions as possible with his young bride. "Mademoiselle, I love you dearly," he wrote to her just before their wedding, "but I shall always love painting more." The two were married just days after Matisse's twenty-eighth birthday.

It was a more than respectable match for the young Matisse, one that satisfied his family and temporarily improved his reputation in his hometown. Amélie and Henri celebrated their wedding with a two-week honeymoon in London, followed by an eighteen-month journey that took them to Amélie's homeland in the south of France, where they stayed for an extended period with her family before a trip to Corsica.

Upon their return to Paris, the couple rented three tiny rooms at 19 quai St. Michel. Matisse celebrated by putting his name in the Paris commercial directory under "Artist," a brash move for the as-yet unsuccessful painter. The increased size of their lodgings was important to the growing Matisse family, which included three children by 1900, but the painter's favorite feature of the fifth-floor studio was the two windows looking directly across to Ile de la Cité.

Through an Open Window in Paris

The studio at 19 quai St. Michel gave Matisse a spectacular view of Paris. Here he began a tradition that would last throughout his career and become one of the more iconic aspects of his legacy. In nearly every place he worked, Matisse painted the view from his studio window, with the window itself as the painting's frame. These images are not photograph-like studies; they do not necessarily replicate the view. Instead, they are impressions of the view filtered through the imagination of the artist.

Notre-Dame (c. 1900).

The view of Notre-Dame Cathedral from near Matisse's studio at 19 quai St. Michel.

Faith and Perseverance

Gustave Moreau succumbed to cancer during Matisse's honeymoon journey, and the struggling painter missed his mentor deeply when he returned to the Ecole des Beaux-Arts to resume his studies. Looking for a new teacher, Matisse attended a class taught by Fernand-Anne Cormon, a painter and instructor whose former students included van Gogh and Toulouse-Lautrec.

During the model's break, when the students usually showed the teacher the work they were doing outside the studio, Matisse set on his easel a painting of a sunset done from his window on the Quai St. Michel. Cormon studied the painting for a few minutes without saying a word. Then he called over his assistant and spoke in a low voice. After the teacher left, the assistant approached Matisse: "I'm truly sorry to have to tell you this, but the boss asked me your age. I told him thirty, and he said you must leave."

Matisse did not return to the Ecole des Beaux-Arts after the incident, and his departure surprised no one. The gap between the type of work he was producing and the accepted standards of art was so huge that he had no choice but to cut his last ties with the Beaux-Arts and the official salons. He was now, in spirit and in very practical terms, one of the Indépendants.

When the news of this latest development in his son's life reached Henri Sr. in Bohain, he sent word that he could no longer finance his son's failure and would cut off the small allowance of a hundred francs a month that had been Matisse's main source of support. Unfortunately, Amélie's family was unable to supplement the income of the newlyweds; a public scandal involving her father's employer had left them financially ruined.

Matisse's fortunes looked grim indeed. Like many struggling artists in Paris, he often earned a little money selling sketches to tourists, and his connections with other artists helped him acquire short-lived painting work at the Grand Palais during the preparations for the Exposition Universelle of 1900. But he found no steady employment or buyers for his paintings.

Matisse was one of hundreds of artists trying to make a name for himself in Paris at the beginning of the twentieth century, and after ten years he had seen little success. He was thirty years old, a father, and a husband. After a decade of trying, he had yet to succeed, and he knew his time was running out. In a letter to friend and fellow painter Simon Bussy, Matisse shared his crisis of faith:

> I know how arduous and difficult life is for a painter and I've already come to understand what a man who was familiar with the bad sides of an artist's life told me about ten years ago: in order to paint, one must be unable to do anything else. All the same, it seems to me I could do something else, though I'm not sure about that.

"I've completely exhausted my family, and I can no longer count on them," he confided. "Along the way I've created a family of my own, which must count on me absolutely. Perhaps it won't take much to save me. For I'm not stupid enough to think that I'm indispensable to the progress of painting, and all I'm thinking of right now is earning my bread."

Matisse credited a painting by Paul Cézanne with saving him and his career during the lean years in Paris. Unaffiliated and unemployed, Matisse had begun visiting the gallery of the famed Parisian art dealer Ambroise Vollard, who owned Cézannes by the dozens.

Although Matisse was struggling to make ends meet, he paid Vollard five hundred francs and ten of his own paintings for a small Cézanne painting called *Three Bathers*. It cost money that Matisse did not have, but the painting

Paris 1900: The Exposition Universelle

The eyes of the world were on Paris in the first summer of the twentieth century, and the City of Light had never looked more beautiful. Paris was once again hosting the World's Fair, known as the Exposition Universelle, and more than nine million visitors from around the world traveled to see the multitude of scientific, artistic, and cultural exhibits from more than fifty different countries. Organizers of the 1900 exhibition decided to forgo the scientific emphasis that had made the 1889 version such a success, choosing instead to celebrate the pleasures of the senses with the theme "Paris: Capital of the Civilized World."

Decoration, style, and luxury replaced Eiffel-style engineering as the focus of the event, even in a place as modern as the newly opened underground rail system, the Métro, where the entrances were marked with elaborate Art Nouveau signs by Hector Guimard. And although the scientific achievements of Louis Pasteur and Marie Curie were applauded, the exhibits along the Champs de Mars that drew the largest crowds were the Palace of Fashion, the Pavilion of Decorative Arts, and the Palace of Women.

From the Eiffel Tower to Les Invalides, visitors could wander through the many exhibit halls and view the wonders of the modern world. Culture was also on display that summer. In addition to a number of theater and musical debuts, two new buildings had been erected specifically to house fine art. ❽ **The Petit Palais, Avenue**

The Great Palace.   PARIS. — LE GRAND PALAIS.   Der grosse Palast.

Grand Palais, circa 1900.

Winston Churchill, housed a French retrospective of fine arts and crafts created through 1800. Directly across the street, ❷ **the Grand Palais, 3 avenue du Général Eisenhower,** housed the Centennial Exhibition of French Art, 1800–1899, as well as the Decennial International Exhibition of Fine Arts, 1890–1900—the largest art exhibition ever assembled.

An imposing classical stone facade with a riot of Art Nouveau ironwork decorates the front of the Grand Palais, and ornate columns draped with oak and laurel leaves surround the building. Over the main entrance are three arches, each divided by double columns. At the base stand statues personifying architecture, painting, sculpture, and music. Juxtaposed against this classical facade is a magnificent domed roof made entirely of curved glass and steel beams. At night the glowing lights from within are projected through the glass panels and into the Parisian sky.

While the public swooned over this luminous addition to the City of Light, critics were mixed in their reaction to the architecture. Many modernists objected to the garish facade; the more traditional reviled the clash of the facade with the modern roof. But most of the critical attention focused on the art exhibits inside.

While the paintings Matisse had submitted for the exhibition had been rejected, visitors to the Grand Palais did see examples of his work. He had been hired as a day laborer to paint garlands of laurel leaves on a mile-long frieze hanging in the Grand Hall. Alongside dozens of others, he hunched over canvases spread on the immense floor, nine hours a day, for one franc an hour, with a boss who did not hesitate to kick in the back anyone he felt was not working up to speed. Matisse was fired after two weeks for insubordination.

provided inspiration that he sorely needed. Amélie understood how much the painting meant to her husband; she agreed to pawn an emerald ring she had received from her mother as a wedding present to raise the money.

Like Matisse, Cézanne had studied law before choosing to pursue painting and had been schooled as a copyist at the Louvre. Although he admired the Impressionists and was briefly aligned with them for a time, he eventually concluded that Impressionism lacked the form and structure necessary for great painting. "I want to make of Impressionism something solid and lasting, like the art in the museums," Cézanne said.

In addition to the freedom to explore colors, Cézanne's example gave Matisse the most basic tenet of nearly all the paintings he would go on to produce. Unlike the Impressionists, Cézanne left nothing to chance. Every

Paul Cézanne's *Three Bathers* (1882) provided Matisse with inspiration for many years.

element of the painting had meaning, and his compositions were so tightly controlled and arranged that every stroke of the painting also had meaning. Matisse had struggled to find a way of heeding Moreau's advice to "simplify painting," and Cézanne showed him how. The secret, Matisse discovered, was to put only the most essential elements on the canvas.

For years, Matisse began each morning in those bleak days in Paris by standing alone in front of *Three Bathers*, contemplating it by the first rays of the sun rising behind Notre-Dame while his wife and children slept. "If I am wrong, then Cézanne is wrong," he would tell himself during these darkest of times. "And I know Cézanne is not wrong."

Years later, Matisse donated Cézanne's *Three Bathers* to the collection at the Petit Palais. Even then, he was reluctant to part with it. He enclosed a note to the curator asking that extra care be taken with the small painting that meant so much to him. "I have come to know this canvas quite well, though I hope not entirely," he wrote. "It has sustained me morally in the critical moments of my venture as an artist; I have drawn from it my faith and my perseverance."

A Journey Always Southward

Matisse had great respect for the traditions of painting that preceded him, and he always considered himself a student rather than a master of art. But he also believed that art should always be moving forward. Unlike most of his instructors and many of his peers, he believed that what had been done well did not need to be done again. He consistently experimented with new styles until he felt he had reached the end of that particular journey.

By 1904, Matisse was earning a meager but respectable income. He had his first successful solo exhibition at Vollard's gallery, and the works he exhibited at the Salon

des Indépendants led to a few positive reviews, including one critic's description of a reworked version of *The Dining Table* as "an ensemble of supple diversity."

It is an irony of modern art history that a man who wanted to make no waves turned out to be one of the most controversial artists of his age. Matisse claimed to never fully understand this label. "What was taken to be boldness was really only awkwardness," he would say

Self-Portrait **(1900).**

about his reputation as a rebel. "So freedom is really the impossibility of following the path which everyone usually takes, and following the one which your talent forces you to take."

The lifelong journey toward light and color began for Matisse when he left home in 1891 and rejected centuries of family tradition to pursue a career as an artist in Paris. After the death of his teacher, Moreau, he left the Beaux-Arts system, rejecting a secure and comfortable, albeit stifling, artistic future. But it was the lessons and freedom he gained from studying Cézanne that convinced Matisse to leave Paris in order to pursue color in its most intense and unfettered possibilities.

Paris may have been the center of the artistic universe at the beginning of the twentieth century, but for Matisse it was simply a point of departure. In the small villages along the Mediterranean coast, far from Paris and the crumbling monarchy of the Ecole des Beaux-Arts, Henri Matisse would boldly pursue his fascination with color. In the process, he would reinvent painting and initiate nearly every new trend of modern art.

Gare d'Orsay

Originally commissioned as part of the Exposition Universelle of 1900, ❽ Gare d'Orsay, 1 rue de la Légion d'Honneur, was a modern architectural masterpiece built to serve the emerging southern rail routes. Part of the station's appeal was the fact that it was designed so that the trains themselves were seemingly invisible. In the station's Main Hall, travelers glided across a vast expanse of marble floor to visit cafés, boutiques, tabacs, or bookstores before descending to the half-lit caves below, where the trains waited to transport the adventurous to their destinations.

Gare d'Orsay was closed on the eve of World War II, though it was used as the depot for returning prisoners of war after the German occupation of Paris ended. For the next forty years, the station sat empty and abandoned. After narrowly avoiding demolition in the 1970s, Victor Laloux's superb turn-of-the-century building reopened in 1986 as the Musée d'Orsay.

Gare d'Orsay, 1900.

Much of the original architecture was retained in the transition from train station to museum, providing a perfect setting for the collection, which begins where the Louvre leaves off. Nearly all the masters of Impressionism, Neoimpressionism, Symbolism, and Art Nouveau can be found in this notable museum, which is itself a remarkable piece of Parisian history.

Chapter 2
St. Tropez
Clarity of Color

The picturesque fishing village of St. Tropez has captivated the imagination of writers, painters, and poets from ancient times to the present. Its charm and beauty remain irresistible.

Paul Signac's *Port St. Tropez* (1899).

In May 1892, artist Paul Signac sailed into the little port of St. Tropez on his prize-winning boat *L'Olympia*. An accomplished sailor and painter, Signac was seeking an escape from the sadness that surrounded him in Paris, where he had recently organized posthumous exhibitions for his close friends Georges Seurat and Vincent van Gogh.

Like those of countless other French artists in the decades that followed, Signac's move to St. Tropez was an attempt to escape the grayness of the North by taking up residence amid the radiant and colorful Mediterranean landscape, with its extraordinary clarity of light. St. Tropez was a village and a view he would praise for the remainder of his life, joining a long list of travelers who arrive and never quite recover from the shock they experience when they first discover its beauty.

"A strange wind pushed me toward the eighth wonder of the world," wrote Signac on arrival in St. Tropez. "In front of me are the golden banks of the gulf, the blue waves coming to rest on a little beach, my beach, below. In the background, the blue silhouettes of Les Maures. I have enough here to work on for the rest of my life. It's absolute joy."

Henri Matisse had wanted to travel to the south of France since his honeymoon trip to Corsica in 1899. "You talk of my going south to the Midi, it is, alas, my dearest dream," he wrote Simon Bussy, who had moved to Menton, a small village between Nice and Monaco. "But, mon cher, without money, what can you do? I think I should work twice as hard there as in the North where the light is so poor—that will be for later, perhaps."

Luck changed for Matisse in the spring of 1904. He had his first successful solo exhibition and great success at the Salon des Indépendants. Additionally, he earned more than a thousand francs from the sale of his paintings. For the first time in their marriage, Amélie and Henri Matisse were ahead of the bill collectors.

Matisse wrote Signac in St. Tropez, asking for advice about finding a place to rent for the summer. He had read Signac's treatise on Pointillism, *From Delacroix to Neoimpressionism*, and had spent months attempting to teach himself the technique. Signac was also vice president of the Société des Artistes Indépendants, and the two began their friendship when Matisse made his first appearance at the Salon des Indépendants in 1904.

The prospect of spending the summer in St. Tropez with Signac appealed to Matisse immensely. He was eager to gain new insight into painting with Signac's help, and he would be doing so in the light and color of the South. For his part, Signac was trying to build an artist colony in St. Tropez, much as Gauguin had done in Brittany and van Gogh had attempted to do in Arles. He was valiantly working to establish a next generation for Pointillism, and he saw Matisse as an important recruit.

Signac found Matisse affordable lodging for fifty francs a month near his own home in a tiny cottage called La Ramade. With two small rooms upstairs and two down, it was not big enough for all five of the Matisses, so Henry and Amélie had to temporarily split up the family. Ten-year-old Marguerite was sent to Toulouse to stay with her mother's sister, and three-year-old Jean was sent to stay with his paternal grandparents in Bohain. Only four-year-old Pierre accompanied his parents south that summer, in part because it was believed that his habitually poor health would benefit from weeks spent in the sea air. Henri, Amélie, and Pierre left Paris bound for St. Tropez on July 12, 1904.

Unearthly Radiance

The Côte d'Azur has captivated the imagination of writers, painters, and poets from ancient times to the present, and travel narratives have itemized its most charming cities and significant monuments since as early as the sixth century. Like so many villages and towns along the Mediterranean coast, St. Tropez has a long and varied history of invasion, destruction, resurrection, and tourism, and its origins are as deeply rooted in myth as is its lingering reputation.

In 68 B.C., an officer of Nero named Torpes was beheaded in Pisa for his Christian beliefs. His head was buried in Italy, but his body was put into a boat with a rooster and a dog that were expected to slowly devour it. The animals apparently had no appetite, and their boat floated to a tiny village inhabited by the Romans known by the name of Heraclea Cacabaria. The headless martyr whose body had drifted to shore was buried in the village; centuries later, Catholic settlers made him their namesake.

Set into the hills just above the curve of a deep bay, St. Tropez rises up the mountainside at the tip of a small peninsula between Marseilles and Cannes. Cut off from the interior by a range of mountains at the foot of the Alps known as Les Maures, and surrounded by the deep blue waters of the Mediterranean on all other sides, the small fishing village is so geographically isolated that an eighteenth-century travel guide considered it "doomed to inevitable ruination . . . certain to be forgotten about."

A visit by author Guy de Maupassant gave origin to St. Tropez's mythology as an artistic and hedonistic paradise. He wrote about discovering the village in an 1887 account of his Mediterranean voyages, and in doing so launched a procession of artists looking for a coastal muse:

> St. Tropez is the capital of this little Saracen realm where almost all the villages built atop steep crags, the better to defend themselves from marauders, are still full of Moorish houses with their arches, their narrow windows and their inner courtyards, home to tall palm trees which now soar above the roofs. St. Tropez is one of these charming, simple daughters of the sea . . . one of those modest little towns, growing in the sea like a shell, nourished by fish and sea air.

The Côte d'Azur is a landscape of dramatic contradictions, where lavender fields, olive trees,

St. Tropez, circa 1900.

windswept salt flats, mountain cliffs, and radiant beaches are all part of the sun-drenched terrain. Traveling to St. Tropez by train likely took the Matisses through much of France overnight. But as light grew in the morning, they would have begun to see the passing countryside of Provence. From the train window, they would have watched as small, boxy houses with pink and ochre walls and tiled roofs, walled cemeteries, deep forests of cypress, chateaux, and vines and olives slipped by in the fog of morning.

St. Tropez was readily accessible only by boat in 1904. Arriving by train as the Matisse family did meant an exhausting journey from Paris, followed by a ride along the coastal railway as far as the port of St. Raphael.

Known as *les tournesols* in French, the sunflowers of Provence dominate the southern landscape and were immortalized by van Gogh's now iconic *Sunflowers*. Originally grown as the source of a cheap alternative to olive oil, sunflowers and their derivative products remain a staple of Provençal culture.

From there it could take up to half a day by a rickety branch line known as the Pine Cone Rail through wild and isolated country, followed by an hour-long journey in a rented boat to reach St. Tropez itself.

Tucked away at the tip of a peninsula, St. Tropez is the only north-facing town on the coast. The blustery northern winds often dissuade those seeking a warm and sheltered winter resort, and the intense heat of the summer means most visitors don't stay long. But the beauty far outweighed the discomfort for Matisse.

"Picture it on a day when the mistral wind is blowing, but also a day when the heat of the sun is so great that there is no discomfort in the wind that brings the chill of the mountain snows from the High Alps

The blue waters of the Mediterranean along the Côte d'Azur.

to the Provençal shore," he wrote. "It is a place of enchanting beauty."

Matisse was mesmerized by the clarity of colors he found in the waters off the coast:

The sea is blue, but bluer than any one has ever painted it, a color entirely fantastic and incredible. It is the blue of sapphires, of the peacock's wing, of an Alpine glacier, and the kingfisher melted together; and yet it is like none of these, for it shines with the unearthly radiance of Neptune's kingdom; it is like nothing but itself, its color is so rich and deep you would think it opaque, and yet it gleams, it is translucent, it shines as if it were lit up from below.

Just a few months before arriving in St. Tropez, Matisse claimed that he had been seduced by a vibrant blue butterfly included in a collection of exotic specimens on display in the window of a postcard merchant opposite the Louvre on the Rue de Rivoli. The butterflies, mounted behind glass on a plaster backing, included one with wings of the same blue that Matisse remembered from his childhood, a blue he had since tried to re-create to no avail using a sulfur flame.

In spite of his efforts to resist, Matisse submitted to temptation and paid fifty francs he could not afford for several of the butterflies, and then eased his conscience by giving them to his wife as a gift. The story of the blue butterfly became a Matisse family legend, symbolizing all the risks the couple took together when young.

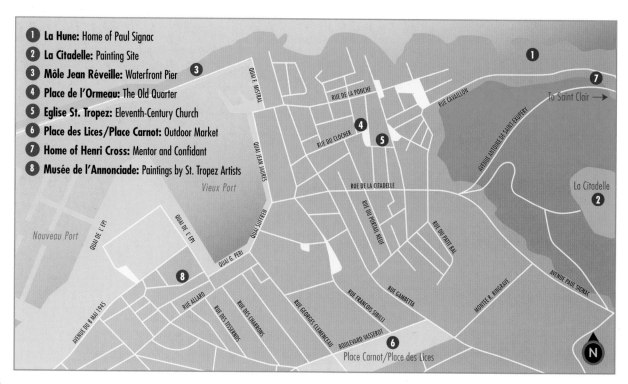

1 **La Hune:** Home of Paul Signac
2 **La Citadelle:** Painting Site
3 **Môle Jean Réveille:** Waterfront Pier
4 **Place de l'Ormeau:** The Old Quarter
5 **Eglise St. Tropez:** Eleventh-Century Church
6 **Place des Lices/Place Carnot:** Outdoor Market
7 **Home of Henri Cross:** Mentor and Confidant
8 **Musée de l'Annonciade:** Paintings by St. Tropez Artists

Standing in the hills above St. Tropez and looking down at the radiant sea, Matisse told Amélie that this was the blue he had been searching for all of his life.

Lost in Pines and Roses

One of the strangest but most prophetic legends along France's Mediterranean coast is that the first incarnation of St. Tropez, the Greek colony of Athenopolis, was founded by Phryne, model for the sculptures of Athena created by the great artist Praxiteles. Phryne was cursed to have the head of a toad, but she was lucky enough to have the most beautiful body of any woman in Greece.

Not coincidentally, Phryne was also a prostitute. And when put on trial in Athens for unseemly behavior, she is said to have lifted up her clothing as part of her defense strategy. The mesmerized jury acquitted her on the condition that she leave Athens immediately and never return.

Eventually she found herself in the Wild West of antiquity—the land of the Ligurians, who since the Stone Age had been building their small, fortified villages on the hilltops of what would become the French Riviera. The beautiful (and veiled) Phryne quickly married a Ligurian chieftain, and together they founded Athenopolis.

But the story has a sad ending. Two years after her arrival and ascent to Ligurian royalty, villagers made a human sacrifice of Phryne in a plea to the gods to keep away foreigners in the future. Alas, she died in vain. Phryne was merely the first in a seemingly endless procession of outsiders to arrive in St. Tropez and reshape it in their own image.

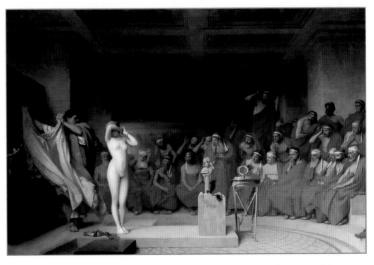

St. Tropez's first tourist and first known human sacrifice, the Greek muse and prostitute Phryne, before the tribunal that sent her out of Greece. (*Phryné before the Areopagus* by Jean-Léon Gérôme, painted in 1861.)

The twenty-year love affair between Paul Signac and St. Tropez had begun when the painter first pulled his small boat into the port. Over the next few years, Signac made his home at ❶ La Hune (The Crow's Nest) in the steep hills above St. Tropez, "five minutes from town, lost in pines and roses." The house had a wild garden and a commanding view of the sea. "As long as I have a little nest for myself and a good mooring for *L'Olympia*," Signac wrote not long after moving in, "all I ask for is the sky, the sea, and the setting sun."

Signac got all he asked for in St. Tropez. The sky, the sea, and the sun setting over the picturesque village below his hillside studio inspired some of his most evocative canvases. Although his Pointillist approach to painting might have been scientific, the result has a tremendous sensory impression. St. Tropez comes to life in these paintings: the wind in the sails of boats leaving

Like most of St. Tropez's buildings, La Hune did not survive the bombings of World War II. This house stands near the site of Signac's beloved home and dates from the same period.

The Gate to Signac's Studio (1904).

port is almost perceptible, and the shimmering roof tiles and glistening water are just as tangible.

La Hune was perched in the hills above town, near the ruins of the ancient ❷ Citadelle, high above town at the end of a road now known as Avenue Paul Signac. The location provides a panoramic view that encompasses the Alps and Les Maures to the west and the Mediterranean and Sardinia to the east. Like so many artists before and since, Matisse set up his easel above the rooftops, in the shadow of the Citadelle. The result was *View of St. Tropez*, a vibrant rendering of a classic subject.

In *The Terrace*, Matisse painted the narrow space in front of Signac's boathouse and its steps leading down to the sea. The painting is drenched in the white sunlight of the afternoon and filled with rambling vines and muted blooms. *The Gate to Signac's Studio* is a similar work that also captures the radiant light of the coast with a decidedly Impressionistic flair. Matisse was particularly fond of these two canvases, and what he described as the "intense white light that is so blinding in St. Tropez." Despite several offers, Matisse did not sell either painting for many years, and *The Gate to Signac's Studio* was a family favorite.

When he wasn't working at his easel at La Hune with Signac or alone in the hills above town, Matisse enjoyed exploring the small streets of St. Tropez, stopping to sketch a particular balcony or boat whenever the urge struck him. From ❸ Môle Jean Réveille, the long and narrow pier that encloses the port, the view remains much the same as a century ago. Matisse spent many hours here sketching the daily activities of the old harbor.

The small village consists of relatively few winding and narrow stone streets that all seem to open into hidden squares and passages seemingly frozen in time. ❹ **Place de l'Ormeau, Rue de la Ponche,** and **Place aux Herbes** are all poetic corners of the oldest sections of St. Tropez, where women carrying fishing nets are as common as those carrying Gucci bags. In a refreshing alternative to the glitzy designer stores found closer to the water, the patisseries, boulangeries, Maison des Papillons, and Café Senequier here have been serving the locals their coffee and petit déjeuner for more than a hundred and twenty years.

Rows of flat and narrow pink, orange, and ochre houses line the twisting and narrow stone streets of St. Tropez, their peeling white shutters pulled closed and latched against the relentless mistral winds. At every turn, balconies drip with bougainvillea, and wisteria vines climb the walls and tumble over rooftops. Above the rows of orange tile roofs looms the bell tower of the multicolored ❺ **Eglise St. Tropez, 21 bis rue de l'Eglise.** Originally built in the eleventh century by local monks, reportedly above the relics of Saint

Signac's La Hune provided one of the most panoramic views of St. Tropez, a vista that many artists, including Signac and Matisse, captured on canvas. At right, the bell tower of Eglise St. Tropez.

Torpes, Eglise St. Tropez has been the parish church of the town's residents since 1554. It has been destroyed and rebuilt throughout the town's tumultuous military history, and the current structure dates to an eighteenth-century Italianate restoration.

In every new place he visited, Matisse spent a significant amount of time exploring local marketplaces. He particularly enjoyed the markets found in Provence and the wide varieties of produce, spices, and delicacies foreign to a Northerner like himself. Behind the rows of yellow and orange houses lining the port is St. Tropez's

The outdoor markets of Provence offer a variety of regional goods to tempt every one of the senses.

oldest outdoor marketplace, ❻ Place Carnot—better known by its old name of Place des Lices—an archetypal slice of Provence that Matisse found irresistible.

Place Carnot is the venue for the markets that still take place every Tuesday and Saturday morning. The thick foliage of the plane trees, the breeze, and the sunshine grace an expansive public square lined with bustling cafes. Here locals erect stalls and sell a wide range of products, including arts and crafts, antiques, produce, cheese, herbs, flowers, and linens, to the delight of residents and tourists alike.

Without a studio of his own in St. Tropez, Matisse could not take advantage of the glorious selection of fresh goods in the Place des Lices markets, which he longed to paint in a series of still lifes. He settled instead for painting the buildings of the marketplace, though he did sketch and write about the market's many temptations.

> In the cool of the morning, beneath the shade of the big trees, there are great hampers of cherries, pyramids of pears, tumbled masses of apricots; the sharp red of tomatoes and the pale yellow of squash add their brilliant notes to this pleasing picture. Carts full of oranges pour their contents out into baskets of every shape, and the golden globes that roll free mingle with white and purple aubergines, like the mighty eggs of some unknown bird.

Matisse arrived in St. Tropez before the onslaught of tourism that would come to define the town but well after it gave up trying to keep outsiders at bay. He was not the first (or the last) artist to find the sights, sounds, and tastes of the mythic village intoxicating and inspirational.

The Only Noble Path

Although Matisse appreciated the company and the conversation Signac provided, he bristled at his host's insistence on a strict adherence to Pointillist principles. Signac's criticism of the large brushstrokes and Impressionistic palette of works like *The Terrace* and *The Gate* caused them to argue frequently about where Matisse's work should be going and who should be determining its direction and destination.

It was during a walk along the St. Tropez shore after one such argument that Matisse produced a quick watercolor of Amélie opposite a tall pine, surrounded by the vibrant oranges, reds, and yellows of the setting sun. The composition centers on Amélie preparing afternoon tea in a small clearing near the shore. Over the next few days, he continued to work on the piece, taking it from

The 1960s' goddess of the French Riviera, Brigitte Bardot.

Too Much of a Good Thing

St. Tropez saw its first tsunami of tourism between the two world wars, when the literary elite of Paris made the coastal village the vacation spot du jour. Apollinaire, Colette, F. Scott Fitzgerald, and Henry Miller are all said to have made St. Tropez a home away from home in the 1920s. Massive destruction during the bombing campaigns of World War II left it a battered and nearly deserted ghost town. It took more than a decade for St. Tropez to be rebuilt as a fair replica of its former self.

The spotlight returned to the small village in 1956 when Roger Vadim shot *And God Created Woman* in St. Tropez, starring his then wife, Brigitte Bardot. After the filming, the sexy young starlet took up residence, thus changing the course of history for this sleepy little fishing village and ultimately the entire area, making the French Riviera synonymous with luxury, glamour, and hedonism.

Thousands of visitors continue to journey to the south of France every year in search of the same light and color that attracted the artists of the early twentieth century, but an even greater number now come to see and be seen on the beaches of St. Tropez. So universal and enduring is its reputation as the playground of the gilded that an estimated one hundred thousand visitors a day pass through the "village" during the vacation months of July and August. "The sheen of sun oil is blinding," wrote a local newspaper in 1962. "By August you can't tell where the tablecloths of the St. Tropez waterfront cafés end and the beach begins, except that the beach has navels."

Things have only gotten worse in the decades since. Today there are far more yachts than fishing boats moored in St. Tropez harbor, and many visitors are more interested in celebrity-watching and shopping in the luxury stores that line the harbor than they are in the town's history. As a result of all this popularity, many French now sarcastically refer to the town as "St. Trop" (*trop* being French for "too much").

The Gulf of St. Tropez (1904).

a watercolor to a series of drawings and then finally to the oil painting *The Gulf of St. Tropez*.

"Since I got here, I have produced only one canvas, painted at sunset, that gives me a little satisfaction," Matisse would write a few weeks later about *The Gulf*. "I still can't believe it was me who did it, although I've carried on working on it in a dozen sessions—it seems to me by accident that I got my result."

Other than Signac and his wife and son, Matisse had no companionship during those long weeks in St. Tropez. Letters from friends scattered along the coast were sporadic, and money was too scarce for him to take small trips to visit artists he knew summering in

other remote coastal towns. Frustrated with his work and bristling from Signac's criticism, Matisse was relieved when painter Henri Cross paid a visit in early September.

Like Signac, Cross was a follower of Pointillism. He was considerably older than both Signac and Matisse, and rheumatism had forced him to leave Paris and settle permanently in the South some years before. But the solitude sometimes became too much, and Cross was always eager to visit with other painters, particularly the young ones whom he recognized as the next generation of talent. He was a good listener, and even the shyest and most reserved artists soon became talkative and confident in his presence. He and Signac were preparing for one-man exhibitions in Paris the summer Matisse visited, and the three reunited several times in Paris that fall.

In the last weeks of their trip, the Matisses frequently made the short journey to La Lavande, a remote coastal village just east of St. Tropez, to visit Cross and his wife, Irma, at their home in ❼ **St. Clair.** For Amélie, the companionship of another painter's wife to confide in and learn from was a tremendous relief. While their husbands wandered the hills around La Lavande, Amélie and Irma sat on the porch of the small pink house, among the vineyards and orchards, enjoying the view and each other's company.

Matisse certainly benefited from the friendship he established with Cross that summer. The two talked at length about life and art and Matisse's decision to turn his back on his family in Bohain and the art establishment in Paris. It was a decision, and a difficulty, that Cross shared. He understood the very real implications of taking such a stand. "I know well that the question of money for survival is disturbing, and constantly gets in the way of the other, higher question," Cross wrote Matisse later that year. "But,

Woman with an Umbrella **(1904). This small portrait of Amélie is perhaps the best example of Matisse's brief Pointillist period. He quickly found Pointillism far too restrictive for his expression of color.**

Musée de l'Annonciade

Not so long ago, residents and visitors to St. Tropez could stand above the town and see only mountain and sea beyond the town's borders. Now the mountains on all sides are nearly covered with rambling villas and vacation condominiums. But it is still possible to see the earlier view through the eyes of the artists who found inspiration here.

With its painted soft pink facade, multicolored mosaic courtyard, and graceful limestone entrance, ❽ **Musée de l'Annonciade, at Place Georges Grammont,** retains the exterior appearance of a sixteenth-century chapel and is one of St. Tropez's most impressive landmarks. Located in the old port, it was originally built as a hospital by the Confrérie des Penitents Blancs (Brotherhood of the White Penitents), whose mission was to care for those injured in Mediterranean fishing accidents.

During the French Revolution the brotherhood apparently fled town, and locals took over the chapel and partitioned it into several smaller spaces used for boat making and repair. The chapel served as a municipal orphanage during the time of Matisse's visit, and, after World War II (with Signac's cooperation and influence), it was renovated completely and converted into a museum.

L'Annonciade Chapel is dedicated to preserving the works of artists who made the town a center of creative expression. Although today's village of St. Tropez often overflows with tourists and jet-set celebrities, inside the Musée de l'Annonciade it is still possible to savor the charms of the old city with its stunning views, charming port, glistening light, and crests of waves, along with the color and warmth of the surrounding landscape. These are captured masterfully in L'Annonciade's collection of paintings by Matisse and his contemporaries who spent some of their most creative days here.

Musée de l'Annonciade.

as you told me, you chose long ago the path of independence, the only noble path."

It was the first time Matisse had received this type of validation. Matisse respected Cross, and

his stamp of approval meant a great deal. The older painter was happy to share his stories, his experience, and his advice with his younger apprentice, and he relished

St. Tropez Muse: Amélie

Amélie Parayre Matisse was a formidable woman who was as fiercely protective of her husband's dreams and ambitions as she was of those of her own children. Visitors to the Matisse "home," a rather grand way of describing their tenement apartment in Paris, were consistently impressed with her ability to create a respectable middle-class household and family from such erratic and unreliable means. Madame Matisse was nothing if not resourceful, and she was totally devoted to her husband's success.

She had modeled for her husband's works since they first met, but the summer of 1904 saw a different type of portrait emerge of Amélie Matisse. In Paris, she posed in the costumes of gypsies and bullfighters; she was one of many props in his elaborate compositions. In St. Tropez, she became his muse.

Amélie is almost imperceptible as her husband paints her in *The Terrace, St. Tropez*, but once the eye recognizes her figure, she is the compelling feature of the composition. Bent over the sewing in her lap, Madame Matisse believes she is hidden from the rest of the world in this private garden, and her intimate dress (a silk kimono) and mussed hair reveal how little attention she is paying to any type of social convention.

The Terrace, St. Tropez (1904).

Her figure flaunts tradition, authority, and expectations again when Matisse places her among the nymphs who seem to be about to join her for a tea party in *Luxe, calme et volupté*. His nonplussed wife is now dressed as a respectable (though still fashionable) Parisian wife and mother should be; at the same time, however, she is serving tea to a party of naked muses, as if she had been expecting them.

the role of teacher. But the relationship was hardly one-sided. Cross felt tremendously energized in the presence of such youthful enthusiasm, and he looked forward to Matisse's visits.

Mythic Landscapes

On the edge of a continent, steeped in classical mythology, huddled around its church, protected by its citadel and wooded mountains, St. Tropez slumbered to the chant of cicadas behind the closed shutters of narrow little houses, all to the delight of those who sought to use it as their muse in painting, prose, and poetry.

Part of the attraction of the Mediterranean coast in the early twentieth century was that it enabled contemporary artists to locate their imaginings of a "golden age" in a real landscape that had played host to the classical idylls of the ancient world. Matisse followed in the tradition of landscape painting while in St. Tropez, but he did so in a particularly modern manner.

Mediterranean landscapes have existed in art since the Greeks first began reproducing images of the places described in mythic literature. In these early works, features of the landscape were not represented in relation to the viewpoint of the observer or a precise visual experience, but were instead based on meanings found in legendary narratives. They expressed ideas more than any actual places.

Artists did not begin depicting landscapes in their own right, separate from the narrative context that gave them meaning, until the fourteenth century, when teachers began instructing their students to paint the landscape as it appears in reality, not memory. "If you want to properly draw mountains and give them a natural look," advised the Italian master Cennini, "take some large stones, rough and not smooth, and draw them from life, bringing in light and shadow as the season dictates."

Luxe, calme et volupté (1904).

These two distinct approaches to what a landscape painting could or should be generated a tremendous amount of debate for the artists of Matisse's generation. Their traditional Beaux-Arts training had emphasized a classical treatment of the landscape as an extension of the allegory, an idyllic setting created in the imagination. So stridently did the traditionalists adhere to this principle, students were actually forbidden from painting outdoors. If the natural world appeared in a composition, it did so strictly in terms of representation.

Bonheur de vivre (1904).

Le *Bonheur de vivre*

Signac's enthusiasm for Matisse's painting came to a screeching halt in 1906, as did his financial and public support, when Matisse exhibited his newest interpretation of mythical landscapes. Although he kept the theme, Matisse made the decision to forgo Pointillist techniques in favor of the bolder and more expressive forms that would come to dominate his oeuvre, a decision that did not sit well with Signac.

Bonheur de vivre is considered by many art critics and historians to be one of the greatest paintings of the twentieth century. This modern interpretation of mythic themes and landscapes looks forward and backward, and says things about art and the hidden energies of life in a way no artist had before. The painting derives directly from the summer Matisse spent in St. Tropez and the influence of Signac, and its mythological theme focusing on the age-old dream of a secret garden free from guilt and worldly care would have impressed even Gustave Moreau.

When it made its public debut in 1906, the painting was profoundly controversial, with critics and artists passionately divided on its merits and Matisse's status as an artist. One of the most enraged was Signac, who announced that Matisse had "gone completely to the dogs. He's taken a canvas eight feet long, surrounded some odd characters with a line as thick as your thumb, and covered the whole thing with flat, well-defined color areas, which, pure as they are, disgust me."

The Impressionists and the Indépendants, on the other hand, were heeding the advice of Cennini and capturing the real texture and color of the natural world in their paintings. In many of Cézanne's compositions, for example, the house, the tree, and the distant mountains all appear with the same force, the same close study, as any object in a still life. Cézanne uses his sensory experience, rather than shared cultural narrative, to dictate his mythic landscapes.

In the months after returning to Paris, Matisse set out to create a landscape based on the themes of the Mediterranean that had captured his imagination in St. Tropez. Still under the spell of Cézanne's *Three Bathers*, Matisse created *Luxe, calme et volupté*, a larger and more mythic landscape based directly on *The Gulf of St. Tropez*, the one canvas that brought him genuine satisfaction from his weeks in the South.

The title *Luxe, calme et volupté* comes from a poem by Charles Baudelaire, "L'Invitation au voyage," about a journey to an imaginary village where cares are unknown and people lead a life of pure pleasure in conditions of luxury and refinement. In the final version of Matisse's painting, laboriously executed in the Pointillist manner, Amélie presides over a picnic on the beach, complete with teacups and saucers, wearing her fashionable hat and contemporary dress, but she has been joined by a group of nude female figures, the Muses themselves perhaps, who seem to have sailed in from another world.

After its debut at the 1905 Salon des Indépendants, Signac proudly and enthusiastically purchased *Luxe, calme et volupté* for his own collection, and it hung in his dining room at La Hune for more than forty years. Critics and many other artists applauded the crowning achievement of this Pointillist work, but Henri Cross accurately predicted that Matisse would not permanently adopt the style. "It is good," he told Matisse, "but you will not remain with it."

The time Matisse spent with Signac and Cross during the summer of 1904 was brief but pivotal. Signac's book explaining Pointillism had made an indelible impression on Matisse in 1899, at a time when he was struggling to find a way forward with his painting. He took to heart Signac's call for "those who will not be content to do over again what has been done already, but who will have the perilous honor of creating a new way of painting and expressing an ideal that is theirs alone." Matisse knew this was the type of painter he wanted to be.

Although Matisse would ultimately fulfill Cross's prediction while gravely disappointing Signac by not staying with Pointillism, the closing lines of Signac's Pointillist text did in fact come to pass in St. Tropez: "The triumphant colorist has only to appear: we have prepared his palette for him."

In the end, Matisse discovered once again that he wasn't cut out to be part of any school or movement, and he moved beyond Pointillism just as he had with Impressionism and his Beaux-Arts training. "One cannot live in a household that is too well-kept, a house kept by country aunts," he would say of that summer in St. Tropez. "One has to go off into the jungle to find simpler ways which won't stifle the spirit."

Indeed, the next summer, Henri, Amélie, and their children would discover Collioure, an even more remote coastal village at the foot of the Pyrenees near the border of Spain. There, Matisse would once again take his painting in a new direction—becoming the leader of Les Fauves, the wild beasts of modern painting, and the first avant-garde artist of the twentieth century.

Chapter 3
Collioure
Perpetual Dazzlement

The bell tower of the Eglise Notre-Dame (on the right) and the walls of the Château Royal (on the left) border the port entrance to Collioure.

The Matisse family spent less than seven months in Paris before boarding a southbound train again. In early May 1905, Henri, Amélie, and the three children departed Paris from Gare d'Orsay bound for Perpignan, the largest town before the border with Spain, where Amélie's sister Berthe had a position as a schoolmistress. After a few days resting and visiting family, they took the train another fifteen miles south to Collioure, in one of the most remote and rugged corners of the French Catalonian coast.

Matisse was thirty-five the first summer he went to Collioure, but he had yet to produce a truly original work of art. He had produced beautiful paintings, and skilled paintings, and provocative paintings—but none that could truly be called his own. Many of his peers elected to spend the summer at La Hune with Signac, but Matisse wanted something new. He had finished his apprenticeships with Impressionism, Pointillism, Cézanne, and Signac; he was ready to strike out on his own. Ironically, the road Matisse took toward Modernism first led him to one of the oldest and most picturesque villages of the Côte Vermeille.

Collioure is nestled between the mountains and the sea, in a remarkable spot where the Pyrenees tumble into the Mediterranean at the border between France and Spain known as the Côte Vermeille (Vermillion Coast). The ocean has almost no surf here; strong waves occur only during rare storms. The sun rises over clear, deep, calm water every morning before setting behind the mountains above town each night.

Although summers can be unbearably hot, the Transmontal wind blows from west to east down out of the mountains and through the streets of the village below in every season, and the cooling breeze pushes the clouds from the mountains out to sea quickly, so light reflects not just off the water but off the rapidly moving clouds as well.

Writing in a 1902 field guide to Collioure, local winegrower Paul Soulier praised the nearly tropical flora, perpetually blue sky, and "climate without winter" of the village, but he reserved his most enthusiastic prose for its luminosity: "It is this intense light, this perpetual dazzlement that gives those from the North the sensation of a new world." Above all, there was an unknown but exotic flavor, according to Soulier, a "je ne sais quoi d'étranger," that gave everyone entering Collioure for the first time "une impression absolument nouvelle."

The sights, sounds, smells, tastes, and textures of Collioure are part France, part Spain, and a little

COLLIOURE
(Pyrénées-Orientales)

Algiers—the result of geography and a long and complicated series of invasions. Henri Matisse was but one in a long line of explorers whose journeys took them to Collioure. As early as 300 B.C., the tiny port was a major stop on the North African trade route. Carthage (modern-day Tunisia) was the major seat of power in the western Mediterranean at the time, and the oldest existing architecture in Collioure is left over from early Moorish settlers.

In the spring of 218 B.C., the great Carthaginian general Hannibal assembled ninety thousand soldiers, twelve thousand horses, and thirty-seven elephants and set out to attack the Romans on their own territory in what would become known as the Punic Wars. Departing from Carthage, Hannibal and his army traveled across the northern coast of Africa and then crossed the sea to "New Carthage," the coast of which would become Spain.

From there, the massive group worked its way north to the snow-topped Pyrenees, where more than twenty thousand soldiers balked at the sight of the mountains and refused to go any farther. Some legends have it that Collioure was founded by a group of these deserting North African soldiers.

Hannibal and his depleted army continued on, across the Pyrenees and through what is now the Languedoc, all the way to the Alps at the other end of the French

The Knights Templar

The Knights Templar began as a small group of pious noblemen dedicated to defending the Holy Land from invaders. Lengend has it that they became the protectors of the two most important Christian relics—the Holy Grail and Christ's Crown of Thorns.

For more than two hundred years, this sect of warrior monks grew in size and strength and eventually migrated to the southern coast of France, where it began to amass tremendous wealth as the creator of the modern banking system. Soon the most powerful kings of Europe found themselves in debt to these mysterious men and began plotting to rob them of their fortune and power.

The Templars were great warriors and builders, and they chose strategic and defensive locations for their fortresses. Collioure is a typical Templar village, with its thirteenth-century castle and military post strategically situated along the coast.

The Knights Templar wore a distinctive white surcoat emblazoned with a red cross.

The Knights were destroyed in a series of battles during the fourteenth century. Some believe the treasures of the Templars disappeared with the defeat of the sect by King Philip of France. Others believe they simply changed their name and adopted a more secretive means of operation—an idea given dramatic play in the popular novel and film *The Da Vinci Code*.

coastline. His defeat there, however, resulted in the fall of the Carthaginian empire. The Côte Vermeille was the first place in Gaul to be settled by the Romans in the first century A.D.; they would later build the Via Domatia road from Italy to Spain, roughly parallel to what is now the A9 highway of southern France leading to Collioure.

Collioure remained a rural Roman outpost until the middle of the eleventh century, when the Knights Templar established a thriving medieval town complete with a chateau, hilltop military base, and cathedral on the site of the old Moorish settlement. Thus the picturesque village emerged once again as

one of the most important ports along the Mediterranean coast.

Despite their tremendous wealth, the Knights were no military match for the armies of King Philip of France. Collioure and the surrounding region, known as Catalonia, were absorbed as part of Majorca in the thirteenth century and as a part of Aragon in the fourteenth. In 1493, the village became part of Spain; under the Treaty of the Pyrenees in 1659, it became part of France and served as the summer retreat of kings until the mid-eighteenth century. The industry begun by the Templars continued to thrive for the locals, who built their life and work around the port.

Strangers in Town

For more than two millennia, strangers arrived in Collioure by boat, though a daring few came by mule along the narrow mountain trails that followed the curves of the rocky coast. Some were simply passing through on their way to somewhere else. Most were in town on business, buying, selling, and trading goods in the port.

The railroad came to Collioure in the 1880s, and a small station was built in the scrublands between the mountains above and the village below. With the

arrival of the train, strangers came to town more frequently, but still primarily for business. The newly built Avenue de la Gare led from the door of the station straight downhill to the busy port.

In 1905, the only accommodations for travelers were at ❶ the Hôtel de la Gare, near what today is 23 avenue Aristide Maillol, a barnlike building just a few steps from the railroad platform. Not much more than a saloon with a few small rooms above, it was run by the Widow Paré, known in the village as Dame Rousette. It had a bar and kitchen, a vegetable garden in the side yard, and chickens and a rabbit hutch in back; the

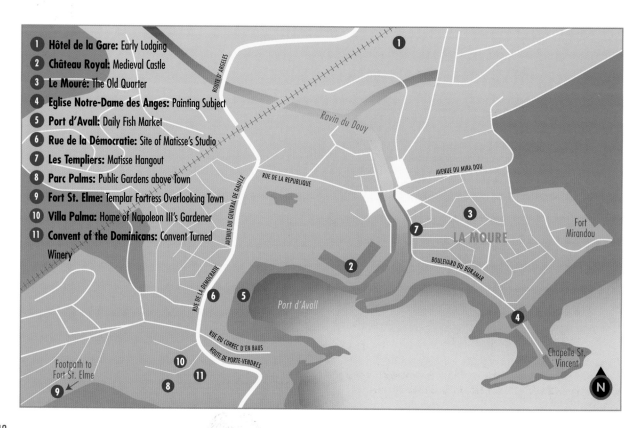

❶ **Hôtel de la Gare:** Early Lodging
❷ **Château Royal:** Medieval Castle
❸ **Le Mouré:** The Old Quarter
❹ **Eglise Notre-Dame des Anges:** Painting Subject
❺ **Port d'Avall:** Daily Fish Market
❻ **Rue de la Démocratie:** Site of Matisse's Studio
❼ **Les Templiers:** Matisse Hangout
❽ **Parc Palms:** Public Gardens above Town
❾ **Fort St. Elme:** Templar Fortress Overlooking Town
❿ **Villa Palma:** Home of Napoleon III's Gardener
⓫ **Convent of the Dominicans:** Convent Turned Winery

occasional guest was the stray sailor or railroad man passing through on the way to somewhere else.

Like most Catalonians, and nearly all the residents of Collioure, Dame Rousette had a general distrust of strangers. Before the arrival of the railroad, outsiders were treated with a certain amount of suspicion in the isolated community: Collioure had had little contact with the world beyond its mountains with the exception of sailors stopping briefly in port.

Matisse and his family stepped off the train in Collioure unannounced and uninvited, and without any real purpose in town that the locals could identify. His fair skin, light hair, and northern accent immediately set him apart from the dark-skinned, dark-haired, Catalan-speaking locals. On the surface, Collioure's emerald mountains, vermilion soil, and indigo sea couldn't be more different from Bohain's dark and treeless

Although the original Hôtel de la Gare, run by Dame Rousette, was long ago replaced by more modern structures, a marker in front of 23 avenue Aristide Maillol indicates the site of Matisse's first summer home in Collioure.

landscape. But Matisse understood the social climate of the small town; he understood the daily lives of villagers working every hour of the day, every day of the week, to make their living. He also understood the pride and aloofness of the community and its wariness of strangers.

Dame Rousette withheld her opinion of Matisse until she was able to completely size him up. He looked funny, acted funny, talked funny, and most definitely painted funny. But he was sincere and polite, absolutely genuine in thought, deed, and action. She liked that in a person. Within a few days of his arrival, Matisse worked out an arrangement with Dame Rousette: one hundred and fifty francs a month for room and board for himself, Amélie, and the children.

Although he was enjoying the time with his family, Matisse longed for the companionship of his peers in Paris, particularly in this enchanting village that was beginning to inspire vibrant and explosive work. On June 25, Matisse wrote and asked his friend André Derain to join him in Collioure. They had met at a van Gogh exhibit in 1901 and, despite their age difference, became fast friends. Derain was ten years younger than Matisse and possessed a freedom of spirit that Matisse sorely lacked. Where the elder painter was critical and lacked self-confidence, the younger was daring and full of bravado.

Matisse had so much faith in his young friend that he and Amélie had traveled to Derain's hometown the previous year—dressed in their most respectable and bourgeois fashions, according to Matisse—in order to convince Derain's parents to continue supporting their son's art career. Monsieur and Madame Derain were so impressed by the couple that they gave their son their full blessing and continued to supplement his income with a living allowance.

"The Dance" of Catalonia

One of the things Matisse admired most about the residents of Collioure was their fierce independence. The geography of the Pyrenees had allowed many of those living along the coast, from the Middle Ages through the Industrial Revolution, to maintain a sense of autonomy from the rulers of France and Spain, who constantly battled over official possession of this territory, known as Catalonia. As early as 1283, Catalonia had its own constitution, and it retained its own laws and customs well into the seventeenth century and the signing of the Treaty of the Pyrenees in 1659.

Catalan language and culture do not enjoy the same official status in France as they do in Spain, but the striped red and yellow Catalan flag can be seen flying in every town, locals still speak the language of their ancestors, and street signs, menus, and advertisements in Collioure are as likely to be written in Catalan as in French.

A key element of Catalan culture is the dance known as the *sardana*, performed by concentric circles of dancers young and old, stepping to the accompanying woodwind band with their joined arms raised high above their heads. The music that accompanies the *sardana* is played by a *cobla*, a band, of twelve musicians playing eleven different wind instruments as well as a double bass. Some versions of the music have lyrics, but most are simply vibrant instrumental pieces used primarily to facilitate the dance. Although the origins of the *sardana* are unknown, the dance has been popular in Catalonia since the Middle Ages and is still likely to be performed in public squares as part of any number of celebrations.

Matisse often recalled watching the dance performed by groups of villagers on the beaches outside his window. When he painted *The Dance* and *Music*, immense testimonies to Collioure's Catalonian colors and culture, Matisse danced around his studio emulating the *sardana*, hoping to capture the rhythm of the concentric circles on his canvas.

The Dance (1909).

Derain arrived in Collioure within a week of receiving Matisse's invitation. The younger painter was good company, but more important, he encouraged joy and freedom and pleasure. Whereas the summer before, Signac had required discipline and science and a personal commitment to the bigger cause, Derain just wanted to live life to the fullest.

Room with a View

Collioure is a fairy-tale village built by knights, ruled by kings, and protected by a castle. With its harbor full of fishing boats, mountainside vineyards, medieval chateau, bell tower, and color-washed houses, it remains a medieval village no matter how modern the era.

Collioure Muse: Marguerite

Of all the subjects Matisse portrayed during his fifty-year career, his daughter Marguerite modeled for the longest duration and with the greatest vitality. Matisse's portraits of her represent an astonishing chronicle not only of his creative invention and stylistic evolution but also of her passage from child to adult.

Marguerite remembered the family summers in Collioure as the most liberating and laughter-filled of her childhood. Running barefoot along the rugged shores with her younger brothers while her father painted his mother, who was seated on a rock nearby, Marguerite never forgot the happiness in Collioure. It contrasted sharply with the tension that could seem so suffocating in their Paris home.

Portrait of Marguerite (1906).

Matisse's 1906 *Portrait of Marguerite* was painted during the second summer the family spent in Collioure, after an afternoon Matisse had spent drawing with his three young children. The portrait was meant to capture the primitive simplicity of a child's drawing by a father who found his daughter to be an invaluable muse.

The portrait was the first gift Matisse would exchange with the painter Pablo Picasso when the two artists met later the same year. And although there are stories of Picasso's friends visiting his studio and using the painting as a target for their darts, Picasso always cherished the portrait of Matisse's daughter. Today it remains with his estate at the Musée Picasso in Paris.

Henri, Amélie, and Marguerite in the Collioure studio, 1907.

Despite its popularity, Collioure is one of the very few coastal towns in southern France that continue to resemble the unspoiled Mediterranean coast that Matisse encountered a century ago. The streets do fill with tourists every summer, but there is no waterside, no miniature golf course, and very few hotels.

❷ **The Château Royal,** first built by the Knights Templar in the thirteenth century, dominates the

The streets of La Mouré.

harbor of Collioure. Much of it was rebuilt in 1659, after the Treaty of the Pyrenees, but it retains a significant amount of medieval structure and style. The original castle walls still curve around the coast and into the mouth of the Douy stream that comes down from the mountains, marking the original entrance to the first port and the heart of Collioure.

A small stone footbridge across the Douy leads to the old quarter of Collioure known as ❸ **Le Mouré,** a maze of dark, narrow streets built into the steep hillside. Maroon, rose, and periwinkle houses squeeze against one another, jutting upward like the rocks on the cliffs below. Here the small shops and family-owned businesses are handed down from generation to generation, and even today most of the town's three thousand residents have family ties in Collioure going back a century or more.

Where the Mouré district meets the coast, buildings curve around a small beach, the Boramar. It is dominated at the far end by the pink and orange bell tower of ❹ **Eglise Notre-Dame des Anges,** at the end of **Boulevard du Boramar.** Although the majority of the cathedral was rebuilt at the same time as the chateau, the village's ancient lighthouse, said to have been built by the Moors, became the cathedral's bell tower and is Collioure's most enduring landmark.

Inside the cathedral are five renowned Spanish Baroque altars created between 1699 and 1720, with intricately carved wooden figures and dioramas of scriptural scenes with delicately painted backgrounds. Matisse and Derain featured the exterior of the cathedral in nearly all of their Collioure landscapes, and sketches of the intricate altars filled their notebooks by summer's end.

Within a few weeks of his arrival, Matisse rented a small space above the Café Olo, on the second of

Collioure's tiny bays, known as ❺ **Port d'Avall.** Although the studio Matisse rented was part of a series of buildings razed and rebuilt after World War II, a row of brightly painted buildings still lines the street, with busy cafés and shops on the first floor and shuttered apartments above. The buildings themselves serve as billboards, with handpainted claims of the best seafood, freshest produce, and finest wine decorating the multicolored exteriors. From his small balcony, Matisse could see past the castle walls and the pink bell tower, straight out to the sea.

The studio above Café Olo that Matisse rented for the summer was located on what is now ❻ **Rue de la Démocratie.** It looked out toward Port d'Avall and had tall French doors that opened onto a small balcony framed by intricate wrought-iron scrollwork. It was only one room—a room so small, in fact, that Matisse had to ask his landlady at the Hôtel de la Gare if he could use her attic to store the supplies and canvases that wouldn't fit in the tiny studio. The morning sun flooded the east-facing room, as did the noise and odor of the port below.

Les Templiers

The most famous of all Collioure cafés, ❼ **Les Templiers, on Avenue Camille Pelletan** in the Mouré district, first opened for business in 1895. Local businesswoman Madame Pou opened what was then called Café des Ports, facing the town market just behind the chateau, as a no-frills watering hole for those doing business in the port. When Matisse and Derain arrived in 1905, the bar was still the local hangout for the fishermen working just a few steps away, and the painters spent some part of nearly every summer evening here.

Madame Pou's son René took over the family business in the 1920s and added a hotel and bar. Soon the many visiting artists who now flocked to Matisse's Collioure replaced local fishermen as Les Templiers' most loyal clientele. Matisse, Picasso, Chagall, Dalí, and dozens of others left artistic tokens of their friendship with the Pou family behind in exchange for dinner, drinks, and lodging at Les Templiers. For decades these original works hung throughout the bar and hotel, until several Picasso drawings and two or three other works were stolen. Now the originals are kept under lock and key, though visitors can see reproductions where the originals once hung.

Les Templiers.

In addition to the extensive collection of paintings, the Pou family also maintained a scrapbook throughout the last century, in which visiting friends wrote good wishes and drew small sketches. *Le Livre d'or* (The Golden Book) was begun by artist Willy Mucha and includes a dedication to both Les Templiers and the village of Collioure: "Pour glorifier Collioure: Dernier lieu des esprits libres, poèts errants, et peintres assoiffés de couleur pure" ("In praise of Collioure: Last place of refuge for free spirits, errant poets, and painters thirsty for pure color"). Matisse contributed a small sketch of a sailboat in 1950, during his last visit to Collioure, the village he described in his entry as "le bonheur des peintres," the joy of painters.

Through an Open Window in Collioure

Matisse began his habit of painting the view from his studios before he reached Collioure, but *Open Window, Collioure* is perhaps the most iconic of his window studies. Painted from the studio above Port d'Avall, Matisse creates a portrait within a portrait, as the open window frames the canvas. Matisse studied this view in a series of sketches and watercolors in which the small curved bay fills the foreground, the ancient bell tower anchors the top left corner, and dozens of colorful Catalonian fishing boats float on shimmering water at the line of horizon.

The final version of the painting depicts the same view, but at this point Matisse begins to incorporate the window itself as a frame for the harbor and the drawing. He pulls the lens back, so to speak, and frames the view with rambling foliage and the iron scrollwork of his balcony, resulting in a tumultuous and celebratory explosion of Collioure's light and color.

In stark contrast to this first window painting in Collioure, Matisse painted *Closed Window at Collioure* on a subsequent trip in 1914. This second work reverses the point of view of the window, showing it from the outside looking into an interior of impenetrable darkness. Critics have long interpreted the work as Matisse's metaphor for World War I, and many now consider it a seminal work in the evolution of abstract painting.

Open Window, Collioure (1905).

Closed Window at Collioure (1914).

Madame Matisse, an ink sketch from 1905.

Port d'Avall was the central business district of Collioure during Matisse's stay. Every morning dozens of fishermen pulled their small boats onto the shore and commenced the ritual of sorting, gutting, and selling their catch. Other boats dumped nets full of anchovies, destined to be stored in barrels of brine for months before going to market. The day's catch was dispersed, fish were gutted and salted, nets were laid out to dry, and boats were cleaned, repaired, and readied for the next night's catch.

Neither visitors such as the Matisse family nor the residents of Collioure would have considered sunbathing on the beach or swimming in the bay, as the crowds today are now eager to do. Not only would the standards of modesty and public decency in 1905 have precluded such an action, but Port d'Avall was in many

ways the town dump, where fish heads and the contents of town chamber pots could be seen floating in the bay until the tide flushed it clean each evening.

A Secret Garden

"Is this still France, or already Africa, with its clumps of agave, and its palm trees dotted here and there among the gardens?" wrote a professor from Paris traveling to Collioure in 1908. "All of a sudden as you emerge on the crest of a hill from a rocky corridor, Collioure! Radiant with light on the curve a small bay, hemmed in by the last burnt foothills of the mountains, a blaze of reds and ochres."

Matisse and Derain explored the steep hillside opposite the Château Royal and Port d'Avall in what is now known as ❽ Parc Palms, the public gardens just below the town's hillside windmill. The wandering trails pass the Convent of the Dominicans, their centuries-old Cave des Vins, and stone houses covered in tropical blooms. The path zigzags through terraces of ancient vineyards, where the two painters would set up their easels early in the morning and work as long as they could, until the relentless sun drove them indoors.

The painters often found themselves on the ancient road once traveled by Hannibal, near the fortress perched on the mountain peak above the town. ❾ Fort St. Elme was built as part of the Templar outpost, with its panoramic 360-degree view offering the perfect vantage point from which to watch for invaders.

After the Templars were driven out, the fortress was abandoned for several centuries. In 1680, it became

Les Vins de Collioure

The Knights Templar began the vineyard tradition in the hills above Collioure in the eleventh century; today, it is still a mainstay of the local economy. The wines of the Côte Vermeille have a naturally high alcohol content, in part because of the crushing heat and the Transmontal wind, which causes the grapes to dry quickly after summer rain. The year-round warm climate virtually guarantees a successful harvest each year.

⑪ The Convent of the Dominicans, just behind Place Orphila, was founded in 1290 and remained a religious feature of Collioure until 1791, when the army took possession of the fortified St. Dominique church and began using it as an artillery depot. The monks continued to harvest the grapes and sell their wines in the small stone Cave des Vins next to the chapel until 1926, when a cooperative of local winegrowers purchased the old convent and turned it into one of the area's most successful wineries.

Local winegrowers were falling on hard times when Matisse arrived. Just a few years before, phlloxera had devastated the French wine trade, and the local vines had just begun to recover. But modern technology was also stomping on the wine tradition. Equipment that made it possible to plant, grow, and harvest grapes more economically and efficiently was simply too large and cumbersome to operate on the steep cliffs. These vineyards had to be tended by hand, and that meant a much smaller profit margin.

Wine is still produced in the area around Collioure.

part of Louis XIV's vast network of property holdings and an important military outpost from which to keep an eye on the Spanish army at the border a few miles away.

In the hills and among the fortress ruins during the summer of 1905, Matisse and Derain painted the landscape, vineyards, and view below over and over again. But it was the discovery of ⑩ Villa Palma, a private residence and secret garden, that gave

The footpath from Collioure to Fort St. Elme.

Matisse the greatest inspiration for his landscapes of Collioure. The luxuriant jungle that is part of the villa was originally created in 1870 by Napoleon III's gardener, botanist Charles Naudin. He collected exotic specimens from such far-flung places as China, New Zealand, Africa, and South America; the plants flourished in the rich soil and Mediterranean climate of Collioure.

Naudin had left Collioure more than thirty years before Matisse arrived, so the gardens Matisse enjoyed were overgrown and ill-tended. The old stone house on the property was rented to a schoolteacher from Perpignan, Ernest Py, who let Matisse set up his easel around the property. Matisse spent hours at Villa Palma sketching the huge eucalyptus and magnolia trees, pepper plants and pomegranates, yellow-flowered cactus, and towering pines.

Py's only restriction was that Matisse was forbidden to enter the house unless the schoolteacher was at home. Py believed it was improper for his unmarried (adult) sisters to have male company unchaperoned.

Today, the gardens are open to the public, though few tourists make the climb to take advantage of the shade or the panoramic view of Collioure below. Naudin's original gardens have long been absorbed into the larger landscape, but exotic and unfamiliar plants still startle and impress those who walk the winding pathways.

The "Wild Beast" in Paris

The Salon of 1905 marked an important turning point in the career of Matisse, establishing him as a painter like none who had come before. The type of painting he invented, the style he would become known for, and the monumental changes in art that would occur as a

Villa Palma, the home of botanist Charles Naudin, provided Matisse infinite inspiration for painting Collioure. The lush gardens are now a public park in the hills above the town.

result all began with this exhibition of four paintings heavily influenced by his summer in Collioure—*Open Window, Woman in a Hat, Woman in a Kimono,* and *Collioure Landscape.*

Matisse returned to Paris in September 1905 with fifteen canvases, forty watercolors, and hundreds of sketches from his summer in Collioure. Immediately, he began work transforming his dozens of studies of Port d'Avall into a large-scale Pointillist landscape. He intended to exhibit the painting in the annual Salon d'Automne and even asked for an extension of the submission deadline in order to finish.

His multiple preparatory works detail the activities of the port below—donkeys straining to pull the weight of full carts, women balancing baskets and pottery on their heads, fisherman repairing nets, an array of sails crowding the bay, and the landmarks that frame them all. But the grueling technical requirements of Pointillism, along with his own need for perfection, dragged the painting's completion beyond the deadline and the committee's patience.

Picasso: Catalonia's Most Famous Son

Henri Matisse was a few years older than Pablo Picasso, and theirs was a friendship based on mutual respect and competition. "From the moment I saw my first Matisse," Picasso explained, "I knew it was a two-man race." Though the men shared the same artistic passion and goals, their individual desires to revolutionize painting took them in two distinct directions. "Matisse is color; Picasso is form," wrote painter Wassily Kandinsky, a disciple of both. "Two great tendencies, one great goal."

Born in Malaga, Spain, Picasso spent several years as the reigning l'enfant terrible of the artistic avant-garde in Paris before discovering the radiant beauty and inspirational capacity of his native Catalonia. Upon seeing the works that Matisse brought back from Collioure, Picasso set out to discover his own El Dorado in the Pyrenees, hoping for similarly explosive artistic results. In 1906, Picasso found Gosol, a remote Catalonian mountain village not far from Andorra, which could be reached only by mule. As Collioure had done for Matisse, Catalonia gave Picasso the lights and landscapes he needed to reinvent art. Picasso visited Collioure on several occasions and for a time settled less than ten miles inland at Céret. Although he was never a member of the Fauve painters who made Collioure legendary, the influence of Catalonia was just as vivid in his work, thanks in large part to the influence of Matisse.

Much has been written about the relationship between Matisse and Picasso, and most of the discussion has focused on a presumed rivalry. In reality, the artists were inspired by each other's work, and each constantly drew on the discoveries of the other to push his own painting forward, while remaining on a distinctly different path. "Apples and oranges" is how Matisse described the pair, though privately he admitted the value of what they shared. "We must talk to each other," Matisse wrote to Picasso near the end of his life. "When one of us dies, there will be things the other will never be able to talk of with anyone else."

Pablo Picasso in 1934.

Although there are numerous preparatory sketches for *Port d'Avall*, the finished painting has never been exhibited publicly. According to Matisse biographer Hilary Spurling, Matisse took the painting home to Bohain to show his mother in the spring. She was not impressed. "That's not painting," she is reported to have told her son, whereupon Matisse took a knife and slashed the canvas.

Unable to complete *Port d'Avall* in time for the Salon, Matisse included a portrait of Amélie that he had done in the weeks after they returned from Collioure, along with several still lifes. The painting of Amélie meets all the requirements for Parisian portraits of the time: the model is dressed as any respectable woman would be, fashionable hat and dress prominently featured, posed in a three-quarter turn facing the artist.

But although the subject matter might have adhered to tradition, Matisse's summer in Collioure had unleashed a use of color that Parisian audiences found shocking and crude. On the opening night of the Salon, a large crowd gathered in front of the painting. Those who weren't laughing at *Woman in a Hat* were soon laughing at the outraged viewers who spit and scratched the surface of the canvas.

The color-drenched canvases Matisse brought back to Paris from Collioure in the fall of 1905 were hung at the Salon d'Automne along with the works of several other contemporary painters who were exploring their own enthusiasm for color. Art historians have described that year's Salon as the first hint of a new and specifically twentieth-century movement in painting, when a group of brash young artists exhibited canvases so exhilarating in color and

Woman in a Hat (Madame Matisse) (1905).

Some of Les Fauves at the 1905 Salon d'Automne, standing near the Donatello sculpture. Matisse is not pictured with his peers; he did not return to the exhibit after opening night.

Romantic sculptor was placed in the middle of the same gallery. Vauxcelles came into the room and, seeing the sculpture, remarked, "Tiens, Donatello au milieu des fauves" ("Ah, Donatello among the wild beasts").

In addition to Matisse and André Derain, Maurice de Vlaminck, Raoul Dufy, Albert Marquet, and Jean Puy were among the painters identified as Fauves, though none actually adopted the term or the premise that Fauvism itself was a fixed set of rules or a "school" in the traditional sense.

Matisse was not bothered by the public or critical reaction, nor did he much notice the crop of Matisse disciples among the next generation of struggling artists crowding the Parisian cafés. Although he would not return to the Salon after that controversial opening night, he never regretted the daring that further branded him as rebellious and outside the artistic mainstream. He was once again turning his back on the easy road, choosing instead to blaze his own trail. He had no time for imitation or imitators. "We belong to our time," Matisse wrote about the critical uproar over Les Fauves sometime later. "We share its opinions, its preferences, and its delusions. All artists bear the mark of their time, and the great artists are the ones in whom that mark lies deepest."

For Henri Matisse, the village of Collioure was more than a new impression—it was an entirely new world. He couldn't have been further, geographically or emotionally, from his family in Bohain; he couldn't have been further, philosophically or aesthetically, from the art establishment in Paris; and he couldn't have been closer to discovering a new form of artistic expression. Matisse returned to Collioure often throughout the next several decades, most often

simplified in design that they came to be known as Les Fauves, the "wild beasts" of painting. Matisse was named as their ringleader.

The art-going public, and the critics who informed public opinion, had a difficult time understanding why and how Matisse was using color in this new, seemingly arbitrary fashion. Younger artists, however, flocked to the exhibit to see Matisse's reinvention of painting. In his calculated use of color, a color more intense and more ingenious than anything painters had managed before, Matisse brought electricity to an art form that had previously set its limits at the warm glow of candlelight.

According to Matisse, the painters never adopted the term "fauve"; it was merely a tag the critics used. It was invented, Matisse said, by critic Louis Vauxcelles at the Salon d'Automne. The entire group had been hung together in Room VII of the Salon. For some reason, an Italianate bust of a child by a

André Derain's *The Lighthouse at Collioure* (1905).

continuing to rent rooms from Dame Rousette when the family accompanied him or staying with friends such as Paul Soulier when he was alone. From his first visit in 1905 to his last in 1950, Matisse found exactly what he was looking for in Collioure—a place of refuge for free spirits, errant poets, and painters thirsty for pure color.

Chapter 4
Nice
An Elaborate Facade

View of Nice and the Baie des Anges.

In the decade following the 1905 Salon d'Automne, Henri Matisse saw a great deal of success and notoriety. Although traditionalists were slow to warm to his vibrant new way of painting, they were unable to stop the tide of Modernism sweeping through Paris. Matisse may have been the first avant-garde painter of the new century, but within a few short years artists such as Picasso, Modigliani, Rivera, and Kandinsky broke nearly all their ties with the formal French art establishment and launched revolutionary styles of painting directly influenced by Matisse.

While he enjoyed the success, Matisse had little in common with this new generation of self-proclaimed bohemian artists living in exile and poverty. Matisse was a good deal older than most of them, married, and the father of three. By 1910, he even had a home in Issy-les-Moulineaux, a fashionable suburb of Paris.

It wasn't only differences in lifestyle that kept Matisse on the outside of the Parisian in-crowd, though. His meticulous and unrelenting dedication to his work afforded him little free time, just as he preferred.

57

Posters such as this one by Charles Leonce Brosse helped to foster Nice's glamorous image.

of Paris, very near the family home, the Matisses once again headed south. After seeing Amélie settled with her family near Collioure, Henri went to Marseille for a quick visit with his oldest son, Jean, who was stationed with his army unit, and then went on to Nice for some much needed rest and time to paint.

Matisse arrived in Nice during one of the most successful and controversial periods of his career. The money his works now commanded was a relief; that much Matisse was prepared to admit. But the exhausting artistic effort and the pressures of success were wearing him down and depleting his capacity to explore the further possibilities of his art.

"I was just emerging from long and tiring years of experiment," he explained, "during which I did all I could to bring these experiments into line with a creation which I wanted to be without precedent." Always one seeking to simplify, Matisse then added, "Yes, I needed to be able to breathe, to relax, and rest while forgetting my cares, far away from Paris."

Nature is the main attraction all along the French Riviera, and the beauty of Nice's landscape is especially dramatic. The startlingly blue water, vast expanse of cloudless sky, rugged terrain, and broad arc of the Baie des Anges (Bay of Angels) are stunning, as is the sprawling city with its ornate villas, red-tiled roofs, palm-lined avenues, and abundance of bright flowers.

The painter may have chosen Nice as a place of restoration, but the city quickly became his most lasting source of inspiration. After one day, he wrote a letter to his wife announcing a new direction in his work. "As for telling you what it will be like," he admitted, "that I couldn't say since it hasn't happened yet, but my idea is to push further and deeper into true painting."

His ongoing wanderlust kept Matisse out of the city as well. Annual family trips to Collioure dominated the calendar, and Matisse made two trips to North Africa during this time. But the onset of World War I put an end to family holidays and trips to foreign lands, at least temporarily. When the war reached the outskirts

At nearly fifty, Matisse was too old to serve in the army. At the beginning of the war, when he'd written a friend who was a high-ranking government official and asked what he could do for his country during wartime, Matisse was told to paint. When he went to Nice alone in the winter of 1917, Matisse found the glittering Belle Epoque gem of the French Riviera to be a shadow of its former self.

Although the majority of the battles were won and lost farther to the north, Nice did suffer the effects of war. Only a few years before, Nice had been renowned as the landscape of luxury, a summer destination of kings and queens; now it was deserted because of the battles raging across Europe, and the local economy, which had become increasingly dependent on tourism, had evaporated as a result.

Welcome to Paradise

Cradled in a small bay where the rocky cliffs of the Alps meet the Mediterranean, this coastal inlet was a natural choice for the series of ports and fortresses that appear at every stage of Nice's history. Like many Mediterranean settlements, it has its roots in the mythology of ancient Greece and Rome.

The colorful houses of Vieille Ville.

For centuries, neighboring kingdoms fought for control of Nice and its strategic location.

Nice is as far to the east of France's Mediterranean coast as Collioure is to the west. And just as Collioure sits beside a mountain range that has been a shifting border between warring neighbors for millennia, so, too, does Nice. Meanwhile, the small villages that lie in the middle of the tug of war have gone on with life as usual.

In 1706, on the orders of the victorious king on the Italian side of the Alps, the hilltop fortifications that for five hundred years had made Nice a formidable coastal bastion were razed, depriving the town of its military value overnight. The little town, now part of Italy, lay nearly forgotten for more than sixty years, until Englishman Tobias Smollett published *Travels through France and Italy in 1766*, "with a particular description of the town, territory, and the climate of Nice."

Smollett was a literary figure of substantial reputation and large following. The first printing of his book quickly sold out, and the book was reprinted three times to keep up with the demand. Excerpts appeared in periodicals around the world, and unauthorized translations appeared in Germany and Sweden, all praising the natural and unspoiled beauty of Nice's landscapes.

"I can scarce help thinking myself enchanted," the normally pragmatic Smollett wrote. "The small extent of country which I see is all cultivated like a garden. Indeed, the plain presents nothing but gardens, full of green trees, loaded with oranges, lemons, citrons, and bergamots, which make it a delightful appearance . . . [and] plats of roses, carnations, ranunculas, anemones, and daffodils,

blowing in full glory, with such beauty, vigor, and perfume as no flower in England has ever exhibited."

By 1780, Nice was renowned throughout Europe as a place with restorative health benefits. The rich and royal from many parts of the globe began fleeing their particular winter hardships and flocking to the glorious warmth of the Midi. The appeal broadened a few years later when Nice became a part of a tradition known as the Grand Tour.

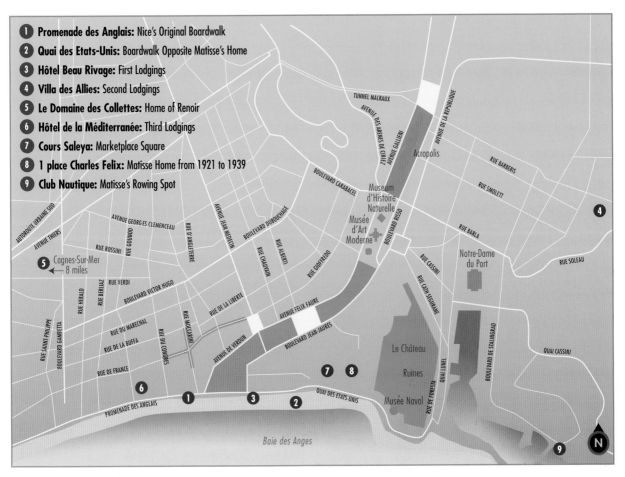

1. **Promenade des Anglais:** Nice's Original Boardwalk
2. **Quai des Etats-Unis:** Boardwalk Opposite Matisse's Home
3. **Hôtel Beau Rivage:** First Lodgings
4. **Villa des Allies:** Second Lodgings
5. **Le Domaine des Collettes:** Home of Renoir
6. **Hôtel de la Méditerranée:** Third Lodgings
7. **Cours Saleya:** Marketplace Square
8. **1 place Charles Felix:** Matisse Home from 1921 to 1939
9. **Club Nautique:** Matisse's Rowing Spot

Promenade des Anglais, circa 1900.

28. NICE — Hôtel Negresco et Promenade des Anglais

Although travelers of all backgrounds have long felt a call to adventure, it was the British upper class who suddenly got it in their heads, around 1800, that a gentleman's education was incomplete until he had toured "the Continent"—until he had seen the Colosseum in Rome, sailed in a Venetian gondola, looked out over Lake Geneva, seen the masterpieces in the Louvre, and, increasingly, visited the Mediterranean paradise of Nice. Within a few years, the village of Nice found itself reborn, with barely a discernible effort on its part, as a tourist destination without rival.

Destination Nice

It is impossible to overstate how much Nice's climate impressed early visitors, especially its winter that really wasn't winter at all. "Strolling there last Christmas," wrote one English traveler in the late nineteenth century, "I recall, the sun was so warm that I lay back at the foot of a lemon tree, on grass sprinkled with flowers the color of violets."

In London it rains approximately one hundred and fifty days a year; in Nice, a mere sixty. Nice receives approximately three thousand hours of sunlight every year; London, a little less than half that amount. Stories about the Riviera's endless summer sparked the imaginations of many nineteenth-century Londoners, who could not wait to make the journey themselves. Nice represented a liberation of the senses that the Victorians found nearly sinful and thus quite irresistible.

In Nice's early days as a tourist destination, most visitors counted on the hospitality of friends, family, or acquaintances or arranged accommodations with local residents. This habit outgrew its practicality by the mid-1800s, with many locals growing tired of the incessant flood of houseguests. The town's entrepreneurs soon found that they could make a tremendous amount of money in the hotel business, and a tourist industry was born.

In 1830, the city listed twelve hotels; in 1850, there were more than fifty; by 1870, there were two hundred. Many of the new hotels had names meant to attract English tourists far from home: Hôtel Victoria, Hôtel de la Pension Anglais, Hôtel de Londres. This idea was also evidenced in ❶ **the Promenade des Anglais,** built as a boardwalk along the sea where fashionable ladies and gentlemen could see and be seen.

Word of Nice's appeal reached the United States after the Civil War, and American tourists soon began choosing Nice as a tourist destination. By 1900, one in every seven guests registered in Nice's hotels was an American. The Promenade des Anglais was extended farther down the coastline, and ❷ **the Quai des Etats-Unis** soon provided the Yanks with a promenade of their own.

A Series of Rooms with Views

Matisse made annual trips to Nice between 1917 and 1921 in a regular seasonal routine. Leaving Paris in early September, he would check into a modest hotel overlooking Nice's Baie des Anges, where he would paint uninterrupted and undistracted for weeks on end. From this period forward, Matisse moved his art indoors more or less permanently. If one of his canvases included a landscape, it would most often be the view from a window—a window that was part of a larger interior.

His working trips to Nice often lasted until early spring. Occasionally Amélie joined him for all or part of the winter, as did their children, who were becoming adults. Most often, however, Matisse found himself, happily, alone in Nice.

Hôtel Beau Rivage

On Christmas Day 1917, forty-eight-year-old Henri Matisse arrived in Nice and took a room at ❸ the Hôtel Beau Rivage, 107 quai des Etats-Unis. Located at the far end of the boardwalk, the hotel was near Vieille Ville, the "old town." His room was so long and narrow that there was room for only a shabby armchair between the bed and the window. But despite their small size, the rooms at the Hôtel Beau Rivage took advantage of the Nice light, and each was dominated by a floor-to-ceiling window that flooded the long and narrow space with a copious amount of sunlight.

When Matisse woke up that first morning, he pulled back the curtains and looked out at a gloomy sea and an overcast sky. The town was cold and deserted. It rained incessantly, making it impossible for him to

Interior with a Violin Case, Nice (1918–19).

work outdoors. Instead, he set up his easel and began painting the view from his window, with the room itself as the subject.

He planned to stay for only a few days before heading back to Paris. A week later, he was still in Nice. When it snowed on his birthday, New Year's Eve, he spent the day indoors painting the view from his window, including the snow and the sea. He wrote a letter to Amélie that day and said it had been so cold that he could scarcely hold his brush.

Blue Villa, Nice (1917).

emotion to canvas. In contrast, the light in Nice is consistently radiant, a trait Matisse craved.

Villa des Allies

In May 1918, the Hôtel Beau Rivage was requisitioned to house soldiers, and all the guests were forced to find other lodging. Matisse and his youngest son, Pierre, rented rooms on the second floor of a small house on the hills rising steeply above and behind the port. Their new home, ❹ Villa des Allies, 136 boulevard Mont Boron, was a small and plain suburban house a twenty-minute walk uphill from the train station. Although far from the life of the city and direct views of the sea, it offered access to several sites on nearby Mont Boron and Mont Alban above the town, where Matisse frequently painted the rambling gardens and orchards in full summer bloom. Their rooms faced west, toward the mountains, and Matisse rose at dawn each day to see the sunrise. "I feel like a human being again," he wrote Amélie on his first day in the new house.

But even in the cold, the radiant city fueled his imagination. "Most people come here for the picturesque quality," Matisse said about Nice years later. "As for me, what made me stay are the great colored reflections of January, the luminosity of the daylight." "I'm from the North," he also said. "When I realized that every morning I would see this light again, I couldn't believe my luck."

In Paris, the skies change dramatically from one season—and sometimes from one day—to the next. The changes in light seriously affected Matisse's mood and inspiration regarding whatever he was working on—disaster for an artist striving to translate

Father and son looked after themselves; visitors were often surprised to find one or the other cooking or cleaning. Matisse's oldest son, Jean, joined his father and brother for a weekend, on a forty-eight-hour leave from his army unit stationed nearby. Matisse wrote a

Le Domaine des Collettes

The new beginning in Nice gave Matisse a chance to reconsider the elements of Impressionism that had had no place in his explosive canvases inspired by Collioure. The proximity of Auguste Renoir, who lived near Nice at ❺ **Le Domaine des Collettes,** in the small village of **Cagnes-sur-Mer,** gave Matisse the opportunity to once again learn from a master.

Like his peers, Renoir had traveled throughout the South during his career, falling in love with the radiance of the landscapes and the light. He visited Cézanne in Aix-en-Provence in the early 1880s and rented his own summer homes in Grasse, Le Cannet, and Magagnosc. Now in his seventies, Renoir had moved more or less permanently to Cagnes, seeking relief from the arthritis that was crippling his body.

In 1907, he purchased Le Domaine des Collettes, also known as Les Collettes. The property came with a small and simple Provençal farmhouse, which suited Renoir well, and also included acres of knotty and robust olive trees, groves of orange trees, and meadows of uncultivated roses and clover.

Matisse visited Les Collettes almost weekly during his months in Nice. Renoir was often his only company outside of hotel staff and hired models. Watching the aged painter struggle to wring every last productive breath from his body, Matisse felt both sadness and admiration. "His life was a long martyrdom," Matisse said after Renoir's passing. "He suffered from the worst form of rheumatism. But as his body dwindled, the soul in him seemed to grow ever stronger and to express itself with more radiant ease."

The little house and rambling gardens retained Renoir's spirit after he died. Matisse continued to visit Les Collettes for years, hoping to capture some of what had inspired his mentor. In 1960, the land and house were accorded the status of historic sites.

Henri Matisse (standing, center) with Auguste Renoir (seated) and his family at Renoir's home, Les Collettes, in 1919.

Despite the wave of modernization that has swept the Riviera, Les Collettes remains unchanged. It retains the tranquility, simplicity, and authenticity that so many artists of Matisse's generation fell in love with in the south of France.

long letter home to Amélie telling her how much it meant to him to spend time with his two adult sons, who would both be in the army by summer's end.

Hôtel de la Méditerranée

Matisse returned to Nice in the spring of 1919 and stayed at ❻ the Hôtel de la Méditerranée, 25 promenade des Anglais. As much as he had enjoyed the house in the hills he had shared with Pierre the summer before, he was alone on this trip and wanted to resume his paintings of the shore. At the Hôtel de la Méditerranée, he again had a view of the bay and the boardwalk. His room was small, but he liked its pretty, Italian-style ceiling, ornate pink tiles, and wooden blinds.

The hotel was not far from the Hôtel Beau Rivage. It was more comfortable, although it was nothing like the luxurious palaces for which Nice is famous: no grand restaurants, ballrooms, or winter gardens. Matisse had a small room, and he had once again managed to pare his life down to nothing but painting. "I'm the hermit of the Promenade des Anglais," he wrote to Amélie, aware how penitential his life looked to outsiders.

His room had large windows overlooking the Baie des Anges. Decorated in a nineteenth-century Italian style, the windows were enhanced with a pretty wrought-iron balcony, long curtains, and wooden shutters to filter out the light. Once again he was facing the sea, in a room flooded with silvery light.

Studio Niçois

By the beginning of the 1920s, Matisse had become somewhat of a fixture in Nice. He was occasionally seen in cafés or bookstores, or simply sitting on a park bench sketching the view. Few tourists who saw the gentleman knew who he was, however. Matisse had

never cultivated his identity as a celebrity. He would more likely have been judged a respectable doctor, on his way to buy his favorite candied fruit at the port or his favorite tea cakes at Gainon's, the city's most famous boulangerie.

Having grown tired of an itinerant lifestyle made up of hotel rooms and train rides, in 1921 Matisse decided to make a permanent home in Nice for himself and his family. After a few inquiries, he found the perfect apartment in the oldest part of the city, near his first rooms at the Hôtel Beau Rivage, with a panoramic view of the sea, the city, and the busy marketplace in the plaza below known as ❼ Cours Saleya.

Cours Saleya had emerged as the center of Nice when the town was rebuilt in the eighteenth century. A typical Italian plaza, it is a long rectangle dominated at its west end by the Chapelle de la Miséricorde. Designed in 1740 by Turin's most famous architect, Bernardo Vittone, the church is a testament to the excess of Baroque sensibilities. At the opposite end of the plaza is the small Chapelle des Penitents Rouges, the private chapel for Niçois fishermen.

Matisse chose an apartment at the opposite end of the plaza, at ❽ 1 place Charles Felix. Originally built in the mid-1700s as the Ancien Sénat, a meeting place for the courts, the villa is a majestic, albeit worn, example of the architecture for which the city is famous. The hard, square lines of the building are transformed by bright colors and ornate embellishments, which soften the imposing tangerine facade that looms over the eastern quarter of the old marketplace.

The market is still held in the square every morning, the calls of fishmongers alternating with those of flower girls, interspersed with the music coming from the cafés lining every sidewalk. The market stalls are filled, day

Cours Saleya market, in front of Matisse's home at 1 place Charles Felix, circa 1910.

1 place Charles Felix today.

after day, with oranges, fennel, and bass fresh from the sea. This is Nice's version of Port d'Avall—and Matisse once again had a ringside seat for the action.

Matisse first rented apartments on the third floor of the building, dispatching Amélie and Marguerite to rental houses and relatives' homes across France to collect the family's scattered furnishings and belongings. The third-floor apartments quickly became cramped, however; for a time the entire space was used as Matisse's studio, while Henri and Amélie took rooms for sleeping at a

nearby hotel. In 1926, Matisse was able to rent the entire top floor of the building, which gave the family both a bigger space and a balcony on the corner of the building with a spectacular view.

Floor-to-ceiling windows grace the top-floor apartments at Place Charles Felix. In addition to offering a full view of the marketplace, the south side of the building opens onto an oceanfront balcony with an unobstructed view of the beach and Nice's most famous landmark, the Promenade des Anglais. Facing both south toward the bay and west toward the city, the apartment at Place Charles Felix afforded Matisse unparalleled exposure to the atmosphere of Nice and the Côte d'Azur.

Dedicated to Work

His new home in Nice gave Matisse an opportunity to establish a work schedule more intense than any he had previously known, but one he'd always striven for. Rising at dawn every morning, he walked to the nearby ❾ **Club Nautique, 50 boulevard Franck Pilatte,** where he exercised by rowing his small boat in the harbor for two hours. During one nine-month period, he went rowing more than a hundred and fifty times and received a club medal for "assiduity," as he put it. After rowing, he returned home to shower, dress, and eat breakfast; then he practiced playing the violin for at least an hour. From 9 a.m. to noon, six days a week, Matisse

worked at his easel. If models were hired, they sat for hours in exacting poses until they could no longer keep from wincing. If they lost the pose a second time, they were fired and sent out the door immediately. A late lunch, light nap, or trip to a nearby café filled the afternoon for Matisse, as did a strict routine of writing letters to his children and friends. At least two hours every day were devoted to correspondence.

By 4 p.m. he was back at the easel again, where he would paint until the last light of day was extinguished. With the row of ocean-facing windows wide open, a strong breeze cooled the apartment as night fell. Twilight was always a favorite time of day for Matisse; from his balcony above Cours Saleya, he could see the sun set behind the mountains toward Cannes and the

Cacophony of Church Bells

Aside from tourism, the most influential aspect of Nice culture is religion. The old Niçois were among the most religious people on the coast. Throughout the winding streets and steps of the old town are tiny squares that seemingly open up out of nowhere, each one featuring its own elaborate chapel. There are hundreds of these small churches throughout Nice, and the ringing of their bells is as constant a sound as the chirping of the cicadas in other parts of the South.

Nice is also still home to religious organizations known as Brotherhoods of Penitents—fraternal organizations dedicated to public demonstrations of "penitence," or philanthropy. Founded in Italy in the fourteenth century during the great Franciscan and Dominican revivals, the Penitents remain a

Niçois chapel in Vieille Ville.

mainstay of Niçois culture. Four of the original seven sects still survive in Nice, all with chapels in view of Matisse's former apartment in Cours Saleya: the Brotherhood of the White Penitents, who care for the sick; the Black Penitents, for the dying; the Blue Penitents, for orphans; and the Red Penitents, for fishermen.

waters beneath his window turn to shimmering gold. When the sun was gone, he would switch to drawing, not leaving the studio until eight or nine, for dinner and then bed.

For Matisse, Place Felix and its proximity to the old section of Nice were a reminder of his days in the Latin Quarter. He felt at home among people who were dedicated to work, to labor, just as he was. While the tourist quarters stood stagnant, life here continued as it had for centuries in the tall old houses jammed together on narrow twisting streets—life that included no piped water, sanitation, gaslight, or heat. Conditions have improved, but balconies in the old city are still just as likely to be draped in the morning's wash as in bougainvillea.

Occasionally Matisse would dine with friends or alone at the restaurant across the square from his apartment. Every few weeks he would walk the short distance of less than a mile to the Ecole des Arts Décoratifs. At the school, run by an old classmate from Moreau's studio, Paul Audra, he would sketch along with the students. Although he lived in Nice longer than in any other place, Matisse remained in many ways a tourist, seldom venturing more than a mile from Cours Saleya unless traveling to or from Paris on business.

Sultan of the Riviera

Just as Monet tended his garden and practically became a horticulturist in order to paint Giverny the way he wanted it, Matisse composed his studio in order to paint it according to his vision. As Matisse

went about creating this world, it is hardly surprising that his studio came to resemble a movie set, with Matisse in the role of director.

In the silent film era, Nice was known as the Hollywood of France, a reputation that grew exponentially when Hollywood director Rex Ingram established his Victorine

The Moorish Screen (1921).

Studios there, primarily for his star Rudolph Valentino. Cinema classics such as *Les Enfants du paradis* (Marcel Carné), *To Catch a Thief* (Alfred Hitchcock), and *Day for Night* (François Truffaut) were filmed at Ingram's Nice studio, as was his classic silent espionage thriller *Mare Nostrum*.

During the 1920s, film crews often outnumbered tourists crowding the boardwalk, cafés, and hotels. "Everything is fake, absurd, amazing, delicious," Matisse declared not long after his arrival, struck by the theatrics of Nice and the mystique of it as a glittering facade.

For years Matisse had collected luxurious fabrics and costumes; when Amélie brought the collection from Paris, the result was a wardrobe department rivaling that of any of Nice's film companies. Matisse also hired local carpenters to construct complex sets on wheels that could be interchanged with a series of platforms and backdrops, and fitted a corner of his studio as an elaborate den of luxury, complete with a richly decorated screen, Arab rugs, and intricate curtains he had brought home as souvenirs from a trip to Morocco.

As in every great city synonymous with fame, young girls hoping to break into show business could be found throughout Nice, waiting to be discovered. Matisse had no shortage of beautiful, experienced models. They dressed up in his luxurious costumes, posed on his makeshift stage surrounded by his exotic props, and became elements in his elaborate facades.

The large, permanent studio gave Matisse the opportunity to produce a series of seductive portraits known as the *Odalisques*. He had become infatuated with the decorative elements of what was then considered Orientalism, and he sought to re-create its exotic blend of textures, patterns, colors, and sensations in his studio. "Orientalism" in Matisse's time was a broad term that encompassed the decorative elements of the Middle East and North Africa, where the female slave known as an odalisque was mythologized as a concubine in the harem of the sultan. The word odalisque originates from a Turkish phrase meaning "for the bedroom."

The results of these elaborate, exotic arrangements were canvases so lush and sensual that when they were exhibited in Paris, Matisse was dubbed "the Sultan of the Riviera." The paintings did not cause a scandal, as so many of his previous works had done, but they did raise serious questions about the future of art and of Matisse himself.

"Matisse is a name that rhymes with Nice," wrote critic Pierre Schneider when the *Odalisques* were exhibited.

> It evokes balconies overlooking the sun-drenched Mediterranean, languishing, lazy odalisques, images of luxury, tranquility, voluptuousness. In any case, as soon as a painter settles on the Côte d'Azur his work is immediately considered to be some sort of summer holiday picture postcard, a sort of perpetual leisure. Matisse: painter of pleasure, Sultan of the Riviera, an elegant hedonist.

To some, it seemed that Nice had tamed the Wild Beast.

Alone at Last

From the time he moved into the apartments at Place Charles Felix in 1921, Matisse considered himself a full-time resident of Nice. For nearly two decades, he barely looked up from his easel. When he did, the world looked quite different. Now that he had established a permanent home for his family, he no longer had the need for it. His sons were grown,

Odalisque with Red Culottes (1921). This is the first Matisse painting purchased by a French museum. It was the first in the *Odalisque* series of paintings, which Matisse worked on for almost a decade in Nice.

married, divorced, and remarried; Marguerite was married and living in Paris; and Amélie preferred living in Paris and being near her daughter to enduring the heat of the South and being ignored by her husband.

As the 1930s came to a close, Matisse was alone with his work, with so few distractions that he could

devote himself entirely to painting—and he did. His years in Nice were the most prolific of his career, and he produced hundreds of canvases. He also had a little time to travel. He went to Italy with a friend, to America to visit Pierre, to Tahiti for adventure, and to Paris once a year to take care of business.

Nice Muse: Henriette

Nice marked a departure for Matisse in his choice of models. With his wife and daughter often elsewhere, Matisse began to hire professional artist's models. Nice had no shortage of qualified and willing applicants, but Matisse was particular about the type of beauty he sought.

Born in 1901, Henriette Darricarrère was one year younger than Pierre Matisse when she was first hired to model for his father. The nineteen-year-old quickly became a substitute daughter for Amélie and Henri at a time when their own children were leaving home. Her family had recently come to Nice in an effort to flee the war; they shared a small apartment near Place Felix in Vieille Ville. Henriette, the oldest child, found work as a dancer and model to support

Matisse and Henriette Darricarrère in the Place Felix studio, 1921.

her parents, brothers, and sisters. They were originally from Dunkirk, and Matisse felt a kindred spirit with his fellow displaced northerners.

Henriette worked six days a week for Matisse for more than seven years, often posing up to ten hours a day except for the two-hour lunch break the entire town observed. Her theatrical experience helped her adopt a variety of personalities to suit the costumes and sets Matisse designed for her. Trained as a ballerina, Henriette had an athletic body and was comfortable in the complicated poses Matisse preferred—lying on a couch or armchair with one leg drawn up and one or both arms raised over her head.

Matisse immediately felt a responsibility to look out for Henriette, and she quickly became a member of the family. She accompanied Amélie and Henri to dinner, to the nearby opera, on country drives, and even on trips to Paris. When Amélie suspected that things were more difficult than usual for the girl's family, she would send bundles of food home with Henriette on the pretense that it was too spicy for the "old people" to eat. When Henriette fell ill, Matisse took her to a doctor.

Perhaps not surprisingly, then, Matisse never forgave his adopted daughter for abruptly running away and marrying a local boy with poor prospects; he even got drunk at a local café with her father to lament the mutual loss of their little girl. Amélie commented that the two were more likely crying over the loss of their workhorse, a remark that earned her her husband's silence for nearly a week.

In the years leading up to World War II, Matisse's Nice paintings were increasingly dismissed as too fluffy, too decorative, too simple. Most notably, they lacked the political agenda the Paris avant-garde was now championing. The frivolity, sensuality, and luxury of the paintings were seen as blasphemous in their lack of seriousness. At the same time, conservative critics and audiences found much of Matisse's new work too graphic and sexual. Although the scenes were completely fabricated and the sensuality was fantasy, conservative thinkers interpreted them literally. Nice was the epicenter of bourgeois luxury, and Matisse had seemingly crowned himself king of it all.

Lydia Delectorskaya assisting in the studio.

Matisse's hedonistic reputation was not helped by Amélie's decision, in 1939, to divorce her husband after forty years of marriage. In many ways she had been viewed as the backbone of the relationship—the partner without whom Matisse's career would surely have foundered. When they split, few questioned who was the guilty party.

Russian-born Lydia Delectorskaya had begun working for the Matisse family as a nurse to Amélie in 1934. For the first year of her employment, Matisse paid little attention to Lydia's presence in the Place Felix apartments, referring to her as "the Russian who looks after my wife," valuable only for her ability to keep Amélie out of the studio so he could work.

As Madame Matisse aged, however, and became less able to keep up with the demands of running her husband's studio, as well as the business of selling, cataloging, storing, and exhibiting his works, Lydia took on more and more responsibilities. Eventually she was running the studio in Nice, hiring models, preparing canvases, and making sure paintings were shipped to Paris or other destinations properly and promptly. She also began to pose for Matisse, and after Henriette's departure she became his most frequent model. Additionally, she ran the affairs of the household, including overseeing the meals and the staff.

Gradually, Amélie came to feel that she was being replaced by a younger, more efficient model of herself. She and Henri were no longer partners in any sense of the word, not even in his career—which she had considered the family business. Jealousy entered their relationship for the first time, and it was enough to end the marriage, which had previously seemed indefatigable. Without any evidence other than her own displacement, Amélie believed until her death that Lydia was also her husband's mistress, a charge the painter and his model always denied.

Rumors began to spread throughout Paris that Matisse had become the hedonist of the Riviera—living a life of luxury; painting his young, half-clad lovers in provocative poses; callously indifferent to the physical and emotional suffering of his wife; and unconcerned with the impending war. Meanwhile, in Nice, Matisse continued to rise at dawn, adhere to his regimented schedule, and push forward with his work. It was the work, after all, that mattered.

Although the end of his marriage was undoubtedly a loss for Matisse, he did nothing to prevent it. He was nearing seventy, and his life had been a series of relationships sacrificed in order to pursue art on his own terms. He knew he was reaping the consequences of the choices he had made long ago, but for him there was no other possible alternative.

"There is only one thing that counts in the long run," Matisse believed.

> You have to abandon yourself to your work. You have to give yourself over entirely, without thoughts, especially without afterthoughts. Only then does your work contain you totally. You also have to forget completely that what you have created—whether it has really been seen or experienced or not—will always be judged by others.

Matisse at his easel, circa 1927.

Chapter 5
Vence
Place of Refuge

While not as popular as other hillside fortified villages, Vence became somewhat of a tourist destination in the 1920s and has always held an allure for travelers.

In the frantic days before the German occupation in 1940, Henri Matisse was in Paris finalizing his divorce paperwork and the distribution of property. As the enemy approached, he fled his Quai St. Michel studio for the safety of the South. It took three weeks of desperate travel by train, borrowed rides in cars with strangers, and nights sleeping in hotel lobbies to get home to Nice, a journey that normally took less than two days. When he finally arrived, he was exhausted and alone.

Amélie and Henri Matisse never spoke again after the divorce, and the bewildered husband continued to proclaim his astonishment at the whole affair. But the children saw things more from their mother's perspective; they knew what it meant to never have their father's full attention, to always come second to his art.

The relationship between Henri and his oldest son, Jean, had been strained for some time, and Jean viewed his father's rumored affair with his mother's nurse as an unforgivable offense. Matisse's younger son, Pierre, now lived in New York, and though the father and son continued their almost daily correspondence, Pierre made it clear that his father should not ask him to choose sides. Marguerite became the family arbitrator, though it was evident that she blamed her father for the disintegration of the family. His oldest child and only daughter had inherited her father's stubbornness, and she remained convinced until the end of her life that he had betrayed both her and her stepmother, Amélie.

Matisse was seventy years old, living through a second world war, and facing his mortality. The hernia that had been so fateful in his youth had flared up on only a few occasions in the fifty years since he had been hospitalized in Bohain, but he had suffered severe abdominal pain steadily since leaving Paris in May.

The last Matisse family portrait, around 1938. Henri and Amélie are surrounded by their three children and their respective spouses, as well as their grandchildren. After 1939, when Amélie filed for divorce, the family did not gather together again until the funeral of the family patriarch in 1954.

Yet he ignored the pain in his abdomen for seven months. By December a tumor had developed, and the risk of heart failure made the situation even graver. Nice was not known at the time for the high quality of its medical services; it had always been treated as somewhat of a backwater by the medical profession. Matisse now found himself in a war-torn country unable to find professionals who could save his life. He asked Lydia to send a telegram to Marguerite begging her to come to Nice immediately.

Within twenty-four hours of her arrival, Marguerite organized a rescue operation using every powerful contact and favor the Matisse name could garner. She had her father removed from the hospital in Nice, over the protests of his doctors, and transferred by train to Lyon, where the distinguished surgeons of the College de France were waiting to operate the moment the painter arrived.

Contrary to the predictions of the doctors and his family, Matisse survived the entire ordeal: the twelve-hour train ride through the Alps and an occupied war zone, the surgery to remove the intestinal blockage, and the two heart attacks that occurred during his first week of recovery. For more than six months he lay in a hospital bed, unable to draw or do much more than turn the pages of a book. Throughout the entire time, Lydia sat in a chair on one side of his bed, Marguerite sat on the other side, and neither spoke a single word to the other.

When Matisse was finally healthy enough to leave the hospital, the question became where would he go. Nice is just over the border from Italy, and speculation was rampant that either the Germans or the Italians would fortify the area to keep the Allies off the Mediterranean coast.

Pierre secured an offer from Mills College in California for a visiting professorship for his father, but Matisse ultimately declined. The job was largely symbolic, and all parties realized it was principally a way to fulfill complicated visa requirements and get Matisse out of France for the duration of the war. Matisse knew he put his life at risk by declining the passage to America, but he chose to stay in France.

Thus, for the first years of the war, Matisse remained in Nice. Too ill to travel, too frail to work, he was not particularly concerned about where the bed he was lying in was located. But the prospect of armies advancing from nearby Italy, coupled with the presence of Moroccan soldiers who had been drafted from the colony and given accommodations in the lobby of his

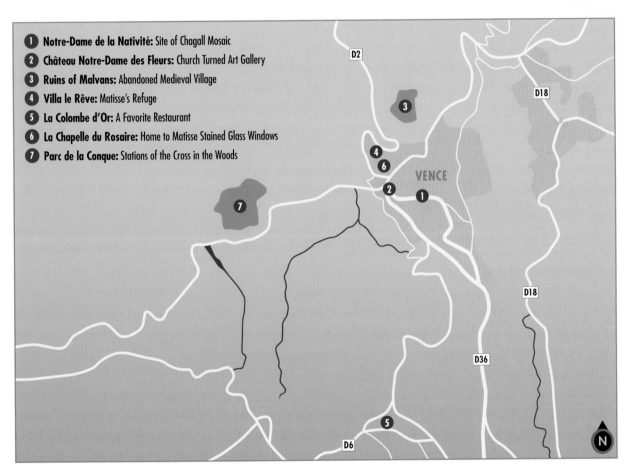

1. **Notre-Dame de la Nativité:** Site of Chagall Mosaic
2. **Château Notre-Dame des Fleurs:** Church Turned Art Gallery
3. **Ruins of Malvans:** Abandoned Medieval Village
4. **Villa le Rêve:** Matisse's Refuge
5. **La Colombe d'Or:** A Favorite Restaurant
6. **La Chapelle du Rosaire:** Home to Matisse Stained Glass Windows
7. **Parc de la Conque:** Stations of the Cross in the Woods

apartment building, finally convinced him to retreat to the safety and solitude of the Provençal countryside. He decided to continue his convalescence in peace just outside the small medieval village of Vence.

Le Rêve de Matisse

Twenty minutes' drive up mountainous and narrow roads from the Côte d'Azur lies Vence, a small and rather unremarkable Provençal village in a region dominated by small and rather remarkable ones. Despite a bloody and often tragic history, Vence has

continued to push forward, emerging from adversity perhaps a bit worse for the wear, but no less able to carry on—not unlike Henri Matisse himself.

Vence officially became a medieval metropolis in 1115, when the count of Provence gave part of his land to Knights Templar crusaders returning from Jerusalem. The monks eventually settled on the land in 1118 and began building a fortress almost immediately.

The cathedral of Vence, ❶ **Notre-Dame de la Nativité,** located inside the town walls in Place

Roads Less Traveled

Along the road that leads out of Vence and into the Alps toward Grasse is ❷ **the Château Notre-Dame des Fleurs, 2618 route de Grasse.** Built as a Benedictine abbey in the twelfth century, converted and enlarged in the nineteenth, the church was a mainstay of Vence religious life for more than seven hundred years. After massive destruction during World War II, the church was sold and briefly became the Museum of Aromas, in honor of the perfume industry centered in nearby Grasse.

In 1992, art dealers Pierre and Marianne Nahon, owners of the Galerie Beaubourg in Paris for twenty-five years, fell in love with the church and surrounding gardens, believing it to be a place charged with history and memories, and the ideal spot for a new approach to art. They relocated the Galerie Beaubourg to Vence.

Although visitors are allowed into the gallery only by appointment, the owners seldom seem to mind if visitors use their parking lot as a point of departure for exploring the nearby woods and their ancient secrets.

A small sign marks the beginning of a worn path leading into the hills above Vence, and back into the past. Near the barren ridge of the Cheiron Range are ❸ **the ruins of Malvans,** an abandoned medieval village where lie the remains of the Templars' fortress, now overrun by wild thyme and lavender. From its perch high above the coast, Malvans once gave its residents an unrivaled view of the translucent blue sea stretching to the horizon and the ominous mountains that become the massive Alps.

The winding Route Tourettes-sur-Loup, through the Alps and toward Vence, circa 1900.

Clemenceau, was originally built in the fourth century on the foundations of a Roman temple to the god Mars. It took its present form in the eighteenth century after devastating battles during the French Revolution.

Although the bell tower is the key feature of the cathedral and the key landmark of the town, the interior holds a multitude of artistic treasures, including forty-nine statues in polychrome wood and a remarkable mosaic by Marc Chagall, *Moses Saved from the Waters,* completed in 1979. Chagall moved to nearby St. Paul de Vence in 1950 and is buried in the town cemetery.

Over the centuries, Vence has changed little either in the character of its inhabitants or in the pattern and rhythm of its way of life. The village survived the Romans, the Goths, and the Saracens. It lived through feudalism, the Black Death, Protestantism, Jansenism, the French Revolution, the Terror that followed, Napoleon, and World War I.

Vence barely blinked when Matisse arrived. In many ways, the realities of war led to a life in Vence that was hardly different than it had been three hundred years before. As the peasants lived by candlelight, Matisse lived by candlelight. As they warmed themselves at olive and pine fires, so did Matisse. He too drank goat's milk and kept it cool in the running spring water outside the kitchen door, often having no more electricity for a refrigerator than anyone else.

An Immortal Village

In the late 1920s, American writer Donald Peattie and his wife, Irene, crossed the Atlantic from New York to Paris with their two children, an infant boy and a four-year-old girl. Two days after arriving in Paris, their young daughter died from influenza she had contracted on the journey. The grief-stricken couple decided that a return to the United States would do nothing to lessen their pain and instead looked to start a new life in the south of France.

Unable to muster the spirit for fiction, Peattie began researching the small medieval village near their new rural home. In 1926, he published the first and only history of Vence, *Immortal Village.* In the book's introduction, Peattie offers a glimpse of a man who finds both hope and redemption in the radiant light of Vence, a man not unlike Matisse during his years at Le Rêve:

Woodcut illustration of Vence, the "Immortal Village," circa 1920.

Those were years so stabbingly felt—so mixed with sorrow—that I cannot write of them. There were hours, too, when my mind was dark with frustration and despair over the failure of my work. Yet the Midi sun poured into my life—an unrelenting friend. It was impossible not to hope, to believe, to take rapture in the daily rhythm of living.

The exterior of Villa le Rêve today, virtually unchanged since Matisse's arrival in 1943.

Lydia discovered what would become Matisse's home in Vence: ❹ **Villa le Rêve, 261 avenue Henri Matisse.** It is a typical country house, with a name that means "the dream." Built in the 1930s for a retired English admiral, the ochre and brown house sits little more than a mile northwest of the medieval walled village in a garden full of pink laurels, yuccas, cypresses, olive trees, and overgrown pines.

Matisse's Women and the War

In 1944, Marguerite was caught working for the French Resistance, crisscrossing the country by train as a courier. Arrested in Rennes, she remained in prison for several months before being put aboard a train bound for a concentration camp in Germany from which few prisoners would emerge alive.

During the journey, an air raid alert sounded and the train was stopped in the open French countryside. A French conductor opened one of the doors and shouted, "Jump and run!" Marguerite was one of the few prisoners who escaped. She hid in the woods of the Vosges for weeks before finally making her way back to Paris. She was forty-six years old.

Marguerite's arrest by the Gestapo led to her mother's arrest and imprisonment. Officers took the clothes Marguerite was wearing when she was arrested and sent them to Paris, along with the keys to the Quai St. Michel apartment. A female agent who matched Marguerite's size and appearance dressed in her clothes and let herself into the house.

Amélie only glanced up from the papers she had spread out on the table as her "daughter" entered the room. In plain view was all the evidence needed to prove Amélie's involvement in the Resistance. She was arrested, served six months in prison, and was released after the Liberation, at the age of seventy-one.

Matisse took the house in large part because of the untamed landscape. The adjacent orchard had been abandoned, and the property was a rambling garden juxtaposed against a tropical landscape of palm trees, ferns, and cactus.

Lydia met with the owner, arranged the terms of the lease, and organized and oversaw the move. When Matisse left Nice and moved to Vence, it was the first time in more than two years that he had left home. Although he was recovering, the aged painter was still frail from his intestinal surgeries and heart failure. He could walk no farther than a few hundred yards, and his digestive system would not allow more than a few bites of food at a time.

In Vence, Matisse wasn't entirely removed from the war. News from Paris was sporadic and letters were often censored, but he continued his daily correspondence with his children and dozens of friends. Air raid sirens made sleeping almost impossible, and when he did sleep, he often had nightmares about what might be happening to Amélie and Marguerite, who were rumored to have been arrested and imprisoned.

On August 29, 1944, American troops entered Vence under the command of General Paul Patch. A firefight ensued, and the fighting lasted several days. Matisse felt well enough to sit at his easel during one of these days, and he barely flinched when German shells exploded in the front yard. Lydia cursed at him in Russian and went to hide in a neighbor's basement. Matisse

Vence still retains much of its medieval atmosphere and architecture.

continued painting, saying he didn't have enough time left on this earth to hide from the war any more.

Matisse made his bedroom and studio at Le Rêve in a large room on the first floor dominated by a fireplace and French doors that opened onto a wide terrace. The

Self-portrait with Panama Hat (1945)

room was sparsely furnished, particularly in comparison with the elaborate and crowded Place Felix apartments. The bed was the only functional furniture, everything else in the room being devoted to painting.

The only possessions Matisse brought from Nice were the souvenirs from his travels that served as props in so many of his paintings. Lydia brought a large trunk to Vence full of fabrics and costumes that Matisse chose for his models to wear. There were also specific items: a Rococo chair, an Etruscan vase, a tobacco tin, a small African carving that he liked to have near. He also brought his cats, Coussi and Minouche, and a few caged doves.

Because of his health, Matisse painted very little after he left Nice, and the few canvases he did produce were the last of his career. In these works he returns once again to one of his favorite themes, producing interiors that feature his bedroom and studio at La Rêve, the large French windows opening onto a terrace, and the landscape and view beyond.

Le Rêve des Autres

In the 1960s, Le Rêve was sold and converted into a school for girls. The exterior was left unchanged, but inside, the large rooms were divided into classrooms and dormitories. Fireplaces were removed, gymnasium-type showers were installed, carpet was laid over the black-and-white marble, and the ceilings were lowered with acoustical tiles.

After the school closed in the mid-1980s, Le Rêve sat abandoned for years; the city of Vence purchased it with the intention of renovating and restoring it. Though licensing issues prevent a formal association with Matisse today, Le Rêve is often rented to groups of artists interested in having the experience of living and painting in the studio, garden, and sunlight that inspired Henri Matisse.

Carving with Color

Although Matisse was ill during his years at Vence, he was far from inactive. His strict discipline in schedule and work were not lost at La Rêve, and he felt an even greater urgency to use what little time he had left. "I told my surgeons in Lyon that I needed three years of good health to complete what I wanted to do," he said

Through an Open Window in Vence

Although he could see the village of Vence from his windows, Matisse seldom walked the short distance to town. Frail health kept him indoors almost constantly, and once again his studio and its windows became elements in his compositions. While his front window gave him a magnificent view of Vence, Matisse preferred the windows opening into the garden. These are his last "window paintings," and they bear the marks of all the others.

The Silence Living in Houses (1947).

In 1947, one of Matisse's last window paintings was used as a travel poster for the city of Nice. The poster, *Nice: Travail et joie* (Nice: Work and Pleasure), was originally printed in an edition of ten thousand. It featured both the window from his studio looking out to the overgrown gardens of La Rêve and the bas-relief medallion of Camille that he had created nearly fifty years earlier in Paris.

The Silence Living in Houses, by contrast, is a dark and sorrowful interior, with an open window looking onto a landscape exploding with color. Interpretation of the painting has been divided. Some believe it reveals Matisse's perception of an oppressive and dark world at Le Rêve. Others, however, believe Matisse is simply extolling the beauty of the Mediterranean light, demonstrating how forcefully it drowns out every other space.

Nice: Travail et Joie (1947).

85

The Clown from *Jazz* (1943).

Icarus from *Jazz* (1943).

in Vence. "I still have things to say that have never yet been said."

Confined to his bed or wheelchair, Matisse needed a new way to communicate color. Unable to manipulate a brush with the precision he demanded, Matisse began to experiment with gouache and paper cutouts. With scissors in hand, he sliced into large sheets of painted paper in order to create his forms, just as a sculptor carves forms from a slab of marble.

Wielding his large scissors, Matisse carved human figures, ornamental shapes, flowers, fish, and foliage. These he placed on a multicolored background until the colors and shapes harmonized to his satisfaction. Some of the cutouts began as models for decorative tiles, pottery, stained glass windows, posters, and magazine covers, whereas others were designed to stand as works on their own. In every case, they are charged with the clarity of color and light that Matisse found only in the south of France.

The cutouts began with *Jazz*, a small "biography" Matisse created primarily out of financial need but also out of creative energy. The book took nearly three years to complete and is a collection of cutout illustrations accompanying text written by Matisse in longhand. The narrative explains the artist's thoughts on art and color, life and choices. Each of the illustrations represents both an iconic image and one that he relates to his "memory of travel." He described the cutouts as incarnations of his thoughts and feelings as well as his sufferings.

Matisse had now simplified art even further, while at the same time pushing it into the future. These were neither paintings nor sculptures; Matisse had fused the two and created something entirely new. What should have, by all accounts, been flat, two-dimensional, uninspired shapes glued to paper had actually come to life. Matisse had managed to create movement using only shape—no tone, no shade, no shadow—just pure color as an expression of an arm, an elephant, a broken heart, or an underwater symphony.

La Colombe d'Or

On the rare occasions when Matisse felt well enough to leave Le Rêve, Lydia would often hire a taxi to drive him the short distance to visit his friend, writer André Verdet, at the famous restaurant ❺ **La Colombe d'Or**, in the nearby village of **St. Paul de Vence.** Matisse enjoyed having tea with Verdet and proprietor Paul Roux on the terrace of the hotel's restaurant under the enormous, ancient fig trees just outside the gates of the walled village.

St. Paul de Vence is an authentic medieval village of winding streets and crooked buildings dating back to the twelfth century. Its sixteenth-century ramparts offer panoramic views over a Mediterranean landscape of fig and cypress trees, red-roofed villas, and the sea beyond. Aspiring and established painters began frequenting St. Paul de Vence during their visits to nearby Nice and Cannes at the beginning of the twentieth century, and the town is now primarily populated by small art galleries featuring local artists and by the throngs of tourists who come for the view and the shopping.

La Colombe d'Or, located in Place de Gaulle, remains one of the most popular (and most expensive) tourist destinations in St. Paul de Vence.

Roux opened La Colombe d'Or just after World War I. He often accepted paintings in exchange for his hospitality from the talented but impoverished artists he befriended. By the time of his death, Roux had accumulated one of the most comprehensive and valuable collections of modern art in the world—including works by Matisse, Picasso, Modigliani, Derain, Braque, Vlaminck, Leger, Dufy, and village resident Marc Chagall.

La Colombe d'Or attracted other celebrities as well. Zelda and Scott Fitzgerald are said to have had a dramatic fight over Isadora Duncan at dinner one night, Jean-Paul Sartre and Simone de Beauvoir were frequent guests, and Yves Montand married Simone Signoret on the terrace.

"I'm not saying that I can bring them perfection," Matisse said of the *Jazz* cutouts. "That would be too much. But I have moments of complete happiness in which nothing else exists for me."

Sister Jacques-Marie

In 1942, seventeen-year-old Monique Bourgeois answered a classified ad in a Nice newspaper seeking a night nurse/companion for an elderly gentleman, who turned out to be Henri Matisse. The painter was recovering from his abdominal surgery and subsequent heart attacks, and Monique helped him through many

The interior of Matisse's Vence studio.

a sleepless night. Like so many of the women in Matisse's life, she also posed for him.

After moving to Vence, Matisse lost contact with Monique, whom he presumed had fled Nice with her family during the invasion. In fact, the young woman had joined an order of Dominican nuns. She became Sister Jacques-Marie, and in an unearthly coincidence, she was sent to a convent in Vence.

Sister Jacques-Marie had harbored an interest in art even before she posed for Matisse, and she was pleased to discover that there were plans to design a new chapel as a replacement for the leaky garage where the nuns currently held mass. She began making small watercolor sketches that she hoped could be used as designs for stained glass windows, should a new chapel be built.

Matisse saw the watercolor sketches when Sister Jacques-Marie showed him her ideas during one of her regular visits to Le Rêve. She explained about the nuns' dream to build a new chapel, and their lack of funds to do so. Matisse quickly became intrigued by the project. Within a few weeks, he had met with church and local officials and drawn up preliminary sketches for the chapel. Additionally, and perhaps more important, he promised to help secure the necessary funds to see the project completed.

In his journal, Matisse tells the story of how the project came to fruition (referring to himself in the third person): "The interest he had found in studying, in musing about the possible stained glass window, in thinking about the need to open up or even overstep his art, his illness, and his old age, all of these combined to make him aware of the new needs, of the possibilities of his art of which he himself had been unaware."

All this excitement about the new project occurred at a time when Matisse was so ill that he spent three-quarters of the day in bed. Lydia covered the walls in his bedroom with large sheets of paper and attached pieces of charcoal to a bamboo pole so that he could sketch his ideas for the chapel. Later he would move to his wheelchair, where he would work to transfer his sketches onto ceramic tiles that would come to cover the chapel walls as murals.

La Chapelle du Rosaire.

With so little mobility, and so few other activities to occupy his mind, Matisse spent the better part of three years obsessing over every aspect of the chapel's final design. No detail escaped his attention—the height of the spire, the marble of the altar, the color and quality of the roof tiles, the embroidery of the priests' robes.

The project officially began when the cornerstone for the chapel was laid on December 12, 1949, two weeks before Matisse's eightieth birthday, and quickly gained attention worldwide. The story of the Sultan of the Riviera being drawn into the embrace of the Catholic Church by a pure young nun made headlines in newspapers, newsreels, and magazines from New York to Tokyo.

Matisse spent nearly every day from 1948 through 1951 working on all aspects of the project, and it was barely completed in time for the June 25, 1951, dedication ceremony. (6) La Chapelle du Rosaire, 468 avenue Henri Matisse, is located on the edge of the mountain, directly across the winding road from Matisse's Le Rêve.

Too ill to leave his bed, Matisse sent the following message to the bishop of Nice announcing the project's completion:

Your Excellency:

I present to you, in all humility, La Chapelle du Rosaire of the Dominican Sisters of Vence. I beg you to excuse my inability to present this work in person since I am prevented by my state of health. This work has taken me four years of exclusive and assiduous work, and it represents the result of my entire active life. I consider it, in spite of its imperfections, to be my masterpiece. May the future justify this judgment.

H. Matisse

La Chapelle du Rosaire

Three sets of stained glass windows are the only source of color in the Chapelle du Rosaire, and it took Matisse more than two full years to execute them from sketch to glass. He was obsessed with the exactitude of the design and the resulting colors that would reflect into the chapel. Using his new technique of paper cutouts, and after numerous preliminary rejected studies, Matisse finally settled on three colors for the windows, the same three colors that dominate the themes and palette of nearly all his canvases: the blue of the sea, the green of the local vegetation, and the yellow of the cactus flower.

Matisse had first seen the cactus flower in Collioure, in the Villa Palma, and the yellow of its blossom and the shape of its leaf became his inspiration in Vence. The plant flourishes in dry areas of the south of France, just as in a desert, and Matisse had long considered it a symbol of life and endurance. He used the pattern of the cactus flower leaves in *The Tree of Life*, the double-paneled window facing the altar.

Along the long southern wall of the chapel is a second set of windows decorated in a vibrant pattern of yellow and blue palm fronds on a green background. The composition of the glass allows the sun to filter through these tall windows and into the chapel at all hours. In the summer, the light through the windows turns the white marble floor into an ocean of blue water teeming with yellow fish. In the winter months, the light reaches all the way across the chapel to the ceramic mural of the Virgin Mother on the opposite wall, showering her in light that ranges from mauve to crimson, depending on the season.

Three large murals dominate the interior of Matisse's Chapelle du Rosaire: *The Virgin Mother and Child, Saint Dominic,* and *The Stations of the Cross.* Each one is made of large white ceramic tiles decorated with thick black lines. "In summary," Matisse explained, "the ceramics are the spiritual essence and explain the meaning of the building."

The Tree of Light illuminating La Chapelle du Rosaire.

For more than two thousand years, Christianity has relied on the primitive icon of the cross as its most enduring symbol. It is nothing more than two perpendicular lines, yet its meaning is unmistakable. That is the exact power and mystique of form that captivated Matisse's imagination and fueled his desire to design the chapel.

The sketches for the *Virgin Mother and Child* mural show that Matisse worked backward on the design. He first drew detailed sketches, then began removing layers of detail. "What can I remove without having the whole thing collapse?" seems to have been his challenge. In the final result, Matisse creates the

A Question of Faith

Raised a Catholic, Matisse never claimed any religious affiliation, never avowed any religious faith, was never known to attend religious ceremonies as an adult, and never created religious-themed works. He claimed no spiritual or religious devotion other than to his art, and he was brazen enough to admit he felt no qualms about taking on a project as reverent as the Chapelle du Rosaire without possessing the least bit of religious reverence. There were complaints about the cost and construction delays, as well as concerns that Matisse's celebrity might overshadow the religious function of the chapel. But the painter's atheism or agnosticism never seems to have been much of a concern—except to Pablo Picasso.

When he came to visit Matisse at Le Rêve in 1948, Picasso was genuinely appalled to find Matisse working on the designs for the chapel at Vence. "Why are you doing this? Do you believe in this or not?" he shouted at Matisse. "If not, do you think you ought to do something for an idea that you don't believe in?"

The two painters spent the better part of the afternoon debating whether an artist could, indeed should, produce art that he or she did not believe in. "I'd approve if you believed what they represent, but you don't," Picasso said as he stood to go, "and I don't think you have any moral right to do them."

Picasso in Nice, 1948.

It was a question, or accusation, that Matisse continued to consider after Picasso returned to Paris. Several days later, he wrote Picasso his answer. "As far as I'm concerned," Matisse explained, "this is essentially a work of art. I don't know if I believe in God or not. I think, really, I'm some kind of Buddhist. But the essential thing is to put oneself in a frame of mind which is close to that of prayer."

The Virgin and Child in La Chapelle du Rosaire.

prototype of the Virgin Mother. Stripped of human artifice, she will never seem old-fashioned because there is no fashion attached to her.

The walls, floor, and ceiling of the chapel are stark. The white ceramic tiles are covered with giant black scribbles that seem like graffiti at first, but it is possible to make out the outline of the Virgin Mother. It takes a minute to adjust to the white light; then the light through the stained glass windows all along the opposite wall becomes evident. This is followed by the slow realization that the room is not white at all; it is actually flooded with color.

Throughout his career, the most monumental and memorable works by Matisse are those that have plucked a mythic female archetype from Mediterranean history and placed her in a contemporary landscape. In Collioure and St. Tropez, he did this with the muses and nymphs that he located on the same beaches where he and his family took tea; in Nice, he transplanted the odalisques of Arabia to the make-believe boudoir constructed in his Place Felix studio.

Matisse did the same thing in Vence with *The Virgin and Child*. When the light comes through the stained glass windows, it is as if she is standing among the palm trees and yellow cactus flowers of the French Riviera. He has taken this mythic female, a very real fixture in Vence history, and placed her in an idyllic landscape that is at once real and imagined. She is real, the palms are real, Vence is real—but all are filtered through the imagination.

The Way of Calvary

In the stony hills southwest of Vence, the oak woods of ❼ **Parc de la Conque, 236 chemin du Calvaire,** are known to contain a circuit of fourteen chapels, or Stations of the Cross, depicting the journey of Christ from the Annunciation to the Crucifixion.

Although the name of the native and fervent artist who created the crude wooden carvings has long been forgotten, the religiously devout in the region have made a ritual of completing the circuit of the fourteen stations as a form of penitence and prayer since as early as the sixteenth century.

So important were these fourteen sculptures to the common people of Vence that they became weapons in the battle between the powerful and the powerless that led up to the French Revolution. On December 20, 1789, the Lord of Vence ordered the Stations of the Cross destroyed and the original wood carvings brought to the public square in front of the Hôtel de Ville. The lord ordered that a huge bonfire be built and the religious objects be burned as punishment for the townspeople's unruly public behavior and outlandish demands for democracy.

Reputed entrance to the secret location of La Conque.

"Let us see how well the wood of Calvary will keep you warm tonight," he said as he lit the fire. Then, according to local legend, the smoke from the burning sacred objects began to suffocate him, and he fell to the ground, gasping his final breath.

New versions of the chapels and the carvings began to reappear in the woods of La Conque some years later, though their exact whereabouts were kept a privileged secret among only the most faithful. Matisse is said to have discovered their location, and came to the woods as often as possible. Those who have seen both say the immense *Stations of the Cross* mural that dominates an entire wall of the Matisse chapel shares many similarities with the Way of Calvary hidden in the woods just outside of town.

The Stations of the Cross in La Chapelle du Rosaire.

Matisse oversaw every aspect of the chapel, including the landscaping, the roof tiles, and the spire that rises from the roof. The small circular mosaic above the window depicts the Virgin Mother giving her son to the world.

The marriage of light, color, and form in the chapel extends beyond the murals. It is in the chairs, the doors, the candleholders, the altar, the confessional, the roof, and the steeple. In essence, the chapel at Vence is a giant art installation, exactly as the artist conceived it. Matisse built a structure that is itself a work of art. He created a

space in which the audience actually enters his art or, more appropriately, enters a state of prayer.

In many ways, the light and landscape of Vence create the art of La Chapelle as much as Henri Matisse did. He studied the variance of light in Vence through the cycle of the seasons in order to determine the depth and tone of the color projected into the chapel, and he adjusted the color of the stained glass windows twice because they did not produce the desired hue when installed. The white walls are the canvas. He has provided the minimalist black outlines. It is the sunlight through the windows that provide the color, and the position of the sun that determines the palette.

With La Chapelle du Rosaire, the art Matisse created is inextricable from the place. Indeed, if the chapel were relocated to any place but Vence, everything about the art would fail.

A Final Burst of Color

The walled city of Vence is isolated and resilient, overlooked by fad seekers, riddled with signs of age and war, and beautiful despite its formidable appearance. It is a place whose history is inseparable from war, Catholicism, and colorful landscapes—the same elements that came to dominate the life of Henri Matisse during the years he lived at Le Rêve.

Vence gave Matisse one last creative burst in a life marked by dramatic explosions of creativity and color. Whether the reason was his recuperation and near total seclusion, the explorations with paper cutouts, or simply the knowledge that time was running out, the work Matisse began at Le Rêve renewed his enthusiasm for color and his desire to push one step further in his pursuit of absolute freedom of expression.

With the war over, his family safely installed at their various homes, and the chapel finished, Matisse made plans to return to Nice. Vence and Le Rêve had served their purpose. Like Collioure, they provided refuge in a time of turmoil to a painter thirsty for color.

"He has lived through an age of world struggle," wrote American art historian and critic Alfred Frankfurter at the opening of a Matisse exhibit at the Philadelphia Museum of Art in 1948. "Yet he has sought only to bring to that world the poetry and joy of nature which its battles have trampled beyond most artists' recognition."

Eighty-year-old Matisse returned to Paris in 1949 for an exhibit of his work at the Musée National d'Art Moderne, and the city was once again shocked. He showed the whole series of work he had completed in Vence: illustrations for *Jazz* and several other books, including Baudelaire's *Les Fleurs du mal* and Ronsard's *Amours*. A few large gouache works were also part of the exhibit, as were twenty-two brush drawings in India ink. Matisse's whole life had been dedicated to the exploration of color, and this major exhibition showed his determination to keep pursuing that passion until the very end.

Matisse, like most of the South of France, indeed nearly all of Europe, had seen better days than those

Matisse photographed in his bed in 1946.

during World War II. But he found a source of inspiration at his country house in Vence that no other place had provided. He liked the sparseness and disrepair, the lack of nosy neighbors, the fabulous view, and the overgrown garden. Le Rêve may have looked like a graveyard of relics, but blossoms were everywhere.

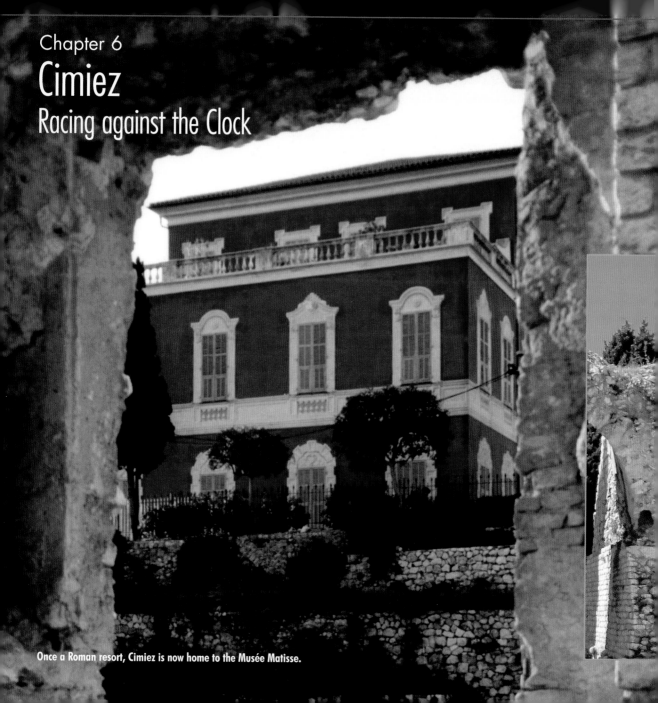

Chapter 6
Cimiez
Racing against the Clock

Once a Roman resort, Cimiez is now home to the Musée Matisse.

By the winter of 1948, Matisse was growing restless with life in Vence. Aside from the day-to-day difficulties of rural life for the elderly gentleman, the large-scale installations for the Chapelle du Rosaire were simply too big to fit inside the studio or any other space at Le Rêve. With the war over and his health somewhat stronger, thanks in large part to the enthusiasm he had for his work, Matisse made the decision to return to Nice.

Matisse's return to city living was actually a relocation to the hillside above Nice and the heights of Cimiez, a place where the painter was hoping to find inspiration from the glorious view of the Riviera below him. In doing so, Matisse chose as his final home on the Mediterranean coast one of the oldest travel destinations in ancient and modern history.

Over the past century, urban sprawl has caused Nice to push its city limits farther and farther outward. With the Mediterranean as an unmovable boundary, Nice has had to expand upward into the bordering mountains. Although it is considered a suburb of Nice today, the ancient city of Cimiez, overlooking the Baie des Anges from its mountainside perch, has held its own against travel trends for more than two thousand years without losing its unique character or history.

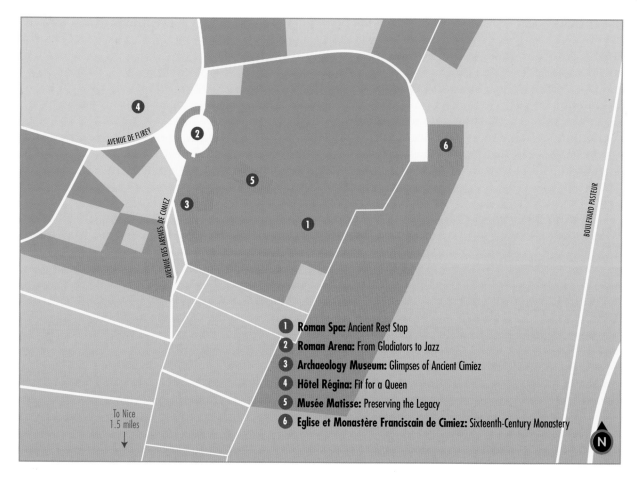

1 **Roman Spa:** Ancient Rest Stop
2 **Roman Arena:** From Gladiators to Jazz
3 **Archaeology Museum:** Glimpses of Ancient Cimiez
4 **Hôtel Régina:** Fit for a Queen
5 **Musée Matisse:** Preserving the Legacy
6 **Eglise et Monastère Franciscain de Cimiez:** Sixteenth-Century Monastery

Historians often refer to the first two hundred years of the modern age as the Pax Romana ("Roman peace") to describe the relative calm that settled over the Mediterranean coast from Syria to Spain right around the time the calendar changed from B.C. to A.D. It was during this peaceful and relatively brief interlude that the ancient city of Cimiez flourished high above a rocky stretch of beach that would someday be known as Nice.

Roman Holiday Inn

An important rural outpost on Via Julia Augustus, the road leading from Rome to Marseille, Cimiez was the last chance to indulge in civilized comforts for the couriers, tax collectors, bureaucrats, and businessmen leaving Genoa on their way to the wasteland known as Gaul. For those same travelers heading in the other direction, on one of the many roads leading to Rome, Cimiez was an ancient rest stop where a weary traveler could find accommodations and comfort lacking in the "provinces." Originally known as Cemenelum, the city was founded by Augustus in 14 B.C. and from the first to the fourth centuries was the capital of the surrounding region, now known as the Alpes Maritime providence.

Cimiez was where ancient travelers could find relaxation, entertainment, a good meal, and a good night's rest. The town featured a renowned ❶ Roman spa, including a steam room, massage tables, and baths of three separate pools of hot, warm, and cold water spread across several hillside acres.

38. - NICE-CIMIEZ. - Les Arènes - Ruines Romaines
Édition Giletta

The ruins in Cimiez have changed little since Matisse's time.

After a day of relaxation, visitors and residents alike often filled the seven tiers of stone seats in the nearby ❷ Roman arena, built to accommodate five thousand spectators, to watch gladiators battle in the elliptical court below. Today the ancient arena is once again a community cultural venue: the Nice Jazz Festival is held on the site each July. Visitors are allowed nearly unfettered access to both the spa and the arena throughout the year. The on-site ❸ Archaeology Museum, 160 avenue des Arènes, contains amazing re-creations of ancient Cimiez and a host of artifacts.

For all the beauty of the town's Mediterranean views, few early Cimiez residents or visitors ventured down the steep hillside to the ocean. Cimiez was already an old city when settlers first began to build crude structures for a port on the shore below. After the fall of the

Roman Empire, the road through Cimiez became less traveled. Eventually, the small and rustic fishing port became the preferred destination, and Cimiez eroded into ancient history. Over the course of the next fifteen hundred years, Cimiez slowly declined into a rural mountainous field, while Nice emerged as the most popular city on the French Riviera.

English writer and traveler Tobias Smollett hired a guide to take him by mule to the ruins of Cimiez when he visited Nice in 1764. In his journal he wondered whether he would see any signs of the intelligent life that once flourished in the otherwise primitive landscape. When he arrived at the mountaintop, he found crops growing in the ruins of an ancient arena, cows drinking from the springs of what were once ancient baths, and a temple being used as a stable for goats. "This land of Roman gods and Julius Caesar," he remarked, "is the same land this farmer now tends. What is it that marks the difference between great men?"

Royal Retreat

Tourism, like all other industries, depends on supply and demand. As the nineteenth century drew to a close, Nice was quickly becoming seduced by its own earning power. Landholders and entrepreneurs were making fortunes in their cooperative efforts with the city to attract tourists. By 1895, there seemed to be an almost frenzied atmosphere in which town leaders worked to keep up with the demand—that is, the many travelers arriving in town willing to pay for just about anything. But some felt that too many of the "wrong" people were now coming to what was supposed to be a retreat for royalty.

According to J. C. Harris, the British consul in Nice, the town was on the decline due to the influx of working-class French and Italians coming to Nice by train for their modest holidays. "I do not want to say, thank God, that there are not still many respectable people in Nice," he wrote to prestigious members of the community and the town council, "but it is also true that you see here quite a number of captains of industry, people of both sexes of more and more blemished reputation, people who affect titles to which they have no right . . . who stay for just a few weeks at the vast, mostly overpriced American-style hotels which have appeared suddenly among us."

At the turn of the twentieth century, popular Parisian magazines such as *L'Illustration* listed dozens of luxury tourist hotels in Nice and Cimiez, including the renowned Régina.

Harris sold city officials on a plan that would restore Nice to its former respectable self and keep the wealthy Brits coming. His solution was to build a model English resort in the hills just above town, far from the crowds of undesirable people below. It was not elitist snobbery alone that gave rise to a reborn Cimiez, however. Nice loved the rich, titled, and famous as much as it depended on them for survival. At a time when gardeners and hotel clerks made two or three francs a day and factory workers made one, a royal family's summer vacation budget of eighty to a hundred thousand francs meant a great deal to the local economy.

Newspapers announced the arrivals of monarchs from Sweden, Norway, Denmark, Holland, and Portugal, and citizens and businesses alike looked forward to their presence. When the news broke that Queen Victoria was looking for a summer destination of rural luxury in 1895, the city of Nice built her one.

Modern Cimiez began with the construction of luxury hotels. To facilitate the transformation, the old dirt road was rebuilt as the wide

The aptly named Hôtel Régina.

Boulevard de Cimiez, which barreled straight up the hill and opened the way for development. The Hôtel Cimiez and the Riviera Palace were grand and glorious monuments to Belle Epoque architecture and excess and rivaled the finest accommodations in Europe's finest cities. Guests were provided with four-times-a-day carriage service down the hill to the seafront, and the hotel offered excursions, including country picnics, exploration of the ruins, and tours of the perfumeries in nearby Grasse. Cimiez also acquired its own post office, telegraph office, banks, and markets, so guests would not need to go "downhill."

The Régina

In 1895, ❹ the Hôtel Régina, Avenue Régina, was built next to the ruins of the arena. The Boulevard de Cimiez from Nice leads directly to its ornate entrance, complete with a sign that would rival any Broadway theater. A private U-shaped drive divides the hotel from a private garden that can be viewed only from the rooms of the Régina above. At the hotel's grand opening, the garden was home to a

The architecture of the Hôtel Régina is a classic example of the garish Belle Epoque aesthetic of the turn of the twentieth century. Multiple cupolas, balconies of wrought-iron scrollwork, and individual atriums dominate the exterior.

dozen peacocks and flocks of imported tropical birds, and even today the occasional flash of color might be a peacock or a parrot briefly escaping the lush enclosed garden.

The wide lobby of the Régina is a breathtaking ensemble of blue marble walls, white marble columns, honey-colored parquet floors, an ornate plaster ceiling, more than a dozen chandeliers, and a grand staircase that splits in two as it breaks away from a wall of expansive windows overlooking a garden. Everything about the building—its location, architecture, decoration, and design—is an exercise in opulence.

Built for Queen Victoria, the Régina commemorated its favorite monarch with a statue of her surrounded by adoring children in the hotel's private gardens.

For the five years before her death, Queen Victoria called the Hôtel Régina her winter home, and its elaborate facade, turrets, private gardens, and astonishing view suited her perfectly. According to her diary, the view from the Cimiez was "marvelous, on the one side the snow-clad Alps and on the other the sea . . . I shall mind returning to the sunless north, but I am so grateful for all I have enjoyed here."

For many decades, the heights of Cimiez held one of the largest concentrations of luxury hotels on the French Riviera, and the crown was the peerless Régina. But hard times returned to Nice and its tourist industry during the Great Depression and the years leading up to World War II. In 1934, the Régina went bankrupt and the wine cellar and exquisite furniture were auctioned off to pay creditors. Three years later, the hotel was transformed into privately owned apartments, just as all the other Belle Epoque palaces of Cimiez would be by 1940.

Henri Matisse originally became a resident at the Hôtel Régina in 1938. He was among the first to acquire one of the luxury apartments created the year before, and he drew the blueprints himself for the construction of a studio that required the demolition of several walls in order to create one large space. Nearly half a decade after its appearance on the hills above Nice, the Hôtel Régina retained its stature as one of the Riviera's palaces, and the painter who often bragged that he lived like a monk was now living like a king.

While the Place Felix apartments in Nice were being readied for the move to the Régina, Amélie Matisse announced her intentions to divorce her husband, so what was originally intended as a home for the couple soon became Henri's alone. His illness and the war interrupted the move, so he did not take up permanent residence at the Régina until he returned from Vence in 1949.

A Factory of Chaos and Color

Matisse's second-floor apartments in the Régina were luxurious, spacious, and filled with light. The large studio featured a center alcove with a floor-to-ceiling bay window, and on either end of the room were two large French doors that opened onto balconies. Beyond these windows were the hills and trees of Cimiez, the roofs of other palatial residences, Nice spread out in every direction, and the blue of the Mediterranean far below.

Matisse moved permanently to the Régina in January 1949 and quickly got to work. The apartment became, in his words, "a factory" with scaffolds, steps, platforms, and crates, all intended to facilitate the movement of an artist who now could barely move on his own. He went from room to room in what he called his "taxi-bed," a bed on wheels with a specially designed tray to hold his tools and a built-in chair to keep him upright.

The final designs, drawings, and sculptures for La Chapelle du Rosaire were rushed to completion in this new space in the days before its dedication; Matisse was too frail to attend the festivities when it was finished in December. Two weeks later, he celebrated his eightieth birthday by quietly sketching his three visiting grandchildren.

Doctors told Matisse he was suffering from cardiac fatigue—not much of an expert opinion, the artist punned, since it was obvious he had "given his heart to the chapel." Jokes aside, his health was rapidly deteriorating, and he suffered from insomnia, breathing difficulties, digestive difficulties, and deteriorating eyesight. By 1951, he could hardly walk, hold a brush, or see.

"I am beginning to take Renoir's place on the Côte d'Azur," Matisse wrote from his Régina studios.

***The Beasts of the Sea* (1952).**

103

He had drawn strength and courage from his visits to Renoir thirty years before and was impressed by the dignity with which Renoir had faced his fast-approaching death. "I have never seen a man so happy," he wrote. "And I promised myself then, that when my time came, I would not be a coward either."

And so he returned to the Hôtel Régina and his pursuit of color, in part out of necessity and in part out of a continued passion. He quickly resumed the large gouache cutouts he had begun experimenting with at Le Rêve.

The Thousand and One Nights, Beasts of the Sea, and *Creole Dancer* emerged from the cut paper, and as they were mounted, movement and color covered every surface of the studio wall.

Visitors to the studios at the Hôtel Régina were often at a loss for words to describe the symphony of chaos and color they encountered. Every surface was littered with stray objects,

Cimiez Muse: Creole Ladies

In that perfumed land, fondled by the sun
I knew—beneath a canopy of trees aglow with crimson,
and palms from which languor pours upon your eyes—
a Creole lady whose charms are unknown to the world.
—"To a Creole Lady," Charles Baudelaire, Les Fleurs du mal

Nice was a cosmopolitan city in the mid-twentieth century, and Matisse was rarely at a loss for girls from varied ethnic backgrounds eager to pose for him in his Hôtel Régina studio. One frequent visitor to Matisse's studio called the endless parade "the models' ballet": an English girl with "changing eyes," a mysterious Turkish woman, a fourteen-year-old Russian girl, a gracious and charming Congolese model, and a smiling Haitian woman were a typical sampling.

Most of the models were acquired by Lydia. She often chose Russian girls, acquaintances of family and friends who needed the money, but just as often the daughter or granddaughter of a visiting duke or prince would sit for the painter, as did neighbors and women who worked as cooks, maids, and housekeepers.

Matisse also drew inspiration from famous women of his time. *The Negress* was a cutout that took up an entire wall in his studio and was inspired by Josephine Baker, the queen of *Les Années folles,* the popular Paris revue of the 1920s and 1930s.

Katherine Dunham.

from a half-eaten sandwich to an eighth-century Chinese vase, and the vibrant colors of the giant cutout murals were so intense that a visiting Simon Bussy declared, "The retina is pushed to the limit of its potentialities!"

"A scattering of color bathes the whole room," wrote an American art student who called on the famous painter at his Cimiez studio in 1951. "It glows like a rainbow, flaring like lightning, becoming soft and supple, then iridescent again . . . blue, orange, violet, almond green, leaf green, orderly, organized, each finding its own shape and place in the ensemble of forms."

American dancer and choreographer Katherine Dunham, who had studied the Creole dances of Haiti in the 1920s, inspired the massive work *Creole Dancer.* In this cutout, Matisse turns the woman into a bouquet exploding with color and movement against a tropical background. The finished work is a brilliant checkerboard of red, blue, pink, orange, black, and yellow against which the dancer's head, skirt, ribbons, and arms swirl in rapid motion.

A few days after its completion, he expressed his satisfaction with the large work. "I think that it has an exceptional quality, and it is both agreeable and useful for me to keep it by me," Matisse wrote in January 1952. "I am not certain that I can do any more work of that quality, in no matter what medium, and for that reason, I want to hold on to it."

Creole Dancer (1952).

The urgency that Matisse had felt all his life peaked in Cimiez. He knew he was racing against the clock, and he fought desperately to continue working for as long as possible. In addition to the cutouts, Matisse continued to design stained glass windows, as he had done for the chapel in Vence. These were mostly commissions for private clients such as the Rockefellers and as a Christmas cover for *Life* magazine. "What counts for me,"

La Gerbe ("The Sheath," 1953).

Matisse said during these frantic months, "is not what I've done, but what I want to do. I would like to be judged only on the whole of my work, on the overall curve of my line of development."

The Journey's End

While Matisse fought to stay alive through color, his family was preparing for the inevitable. Although she never spoke to her ex-husband, Amélie had moved to nearby Aix-en-Provence and was working with Marguerite to locate lost or missing records for an exhaustive family archive she was assembling. When town officials from Le Cateau approached the Matisse family about opening a museum in their little town, where the great painter had been born, they not only obtained Amélie's agreement but also became the surprised recipients of Matisse family records, belongings, and many works of art. All three Matisse children attended the museum's opening, held just after their father's death, and the family continues to support the private museum.

By the end of 1952, Matisse's handwriting had become illegible. This was another in a long line of devastating developments for a man who had devoted several hours every day to reading and writing letters to his family and friends. It also meant he could no longer draw, though he continued to ask for a pencil from time to time in order to attempt a sketch.

Jean Matisse still had only infrequent contact with his father, and promised visits from Pierre in America did not materialize either, though his letters remained intimate and regular. In contrast, Marguerite was a frequent presence at the Régina, though she refused to stay in the apartments as long as Lydia slept under the same roof. She took the train from nearby Aix, where she was living with her mother.

Matisse and one of his many models at La Régina.

In the end, it was Lydia Delectorskaya who remained faithful to Matisse and who helped him through the grueling nights so that he might have another day. Nearly twenty years after she came to work for the family as a nurse for Amélie, she remained his most loyal employee, friend, and family member.

Sister Jacques-Marie, the young nurse and nun who had inspired Matisse to undertake the chapel in Vence, visited him in the fall of 1954, having received word from Marguerite that the painter's health was getting worse. She had always considered Matisse "thoughtful, tender, and solicitous," and it caused her considerable grief to see her old friend in his current condition.

Lydia, photographed by Matisse, 1935.

Muse and Companion: Lydia

Matisse's first painting of Lydia, *Blue Eyes*, came about after he had spent months in bed recuperating from a flu that passed through Nice in the winter of 1935–36, taking many victims in its wake. During a conversation with Amélie, he looked over and saw the nanny sitting with her head leaning on her arms, in a daydream. "Don't move!" Lydia remembered him shouting. "And then, opening the notepad, he began sketching me." After this first sitting, she quickly became one of his favorite models.

For all the blame she received for the breakup of the Matisse marriage, there is no evidence that Lydia had anything other than a professional relationship with the artist, albeit an intensely loyal one. After his death, Lydia published *Henri Matisse: With Apparent Ease*. Although many expected a sizzling confessional, it was instead a meticulous account of how her former employer worked—including extensive photographs demonstrating the evolution of each canvas over time.

In private interviews, Lydia often confessed how difficult it was to work for Matisse, how demanding and unforgiving he could be. She stayed, she said, because she never stopped being awed by his talent, the genius of his work.

During Matisse's years in Vence during the war, Lydia literally kept the elderly and ill painter alive. Her connections on the black market secured them enough food to survive; her stubbornness got Matisse's works to Paris and his dealers so that he might get paid; and her efficiency and keen sense of business kept the house and studio running as if there were no war at all going on outside their windows. At the Hôtel Régina, she continued to do the same.

"I never expected to see him in such a state," she wrote years later. "There was nothing left of him but a poor old man, hunched and huddled. It was as if he could no longer see, and could hardly speak." It is hard to reconcile this version of the artist with the man who continued to work fervently from his taxi-bed.

On November 1, 1954, Matisse finished the design for a stained glass window commissioned by Nelson Rockefeller for the Union Church of Pocantico Hills, New York, in memory of his mother. Originally, Matisse had turned down the project because he was unable to travel to the site of the church to see it in its natural light, which would have helped him determine the best colors for the rose-patterned window. But with the help of Pierre Matisse and the director of the Museum of Modern Art in New York,

Les Souvenirs de Matisser

A short walk from the Hôtel Régina, through the ruins of the ancient arena and the park on the other side, stands a magnificent seventeenth-century Genoese villa known as Villa des Arènes. Its three stories are painted a magnificent crimson, and its more than fifty windows are shuttered in white and green. This is ❺ the Musée Matisse, a glorious and fitting testament to the life and work of an artist who lived his last days just steps to the west and now lies peacefully just a few steps to the east.

Among the most interesting features of the building's exterior are its numerous windows, most of which are part of an elaborate stone facade meant to fool the eye. Not all the windows are real; many are, in fact, paintings. The facade has included this "trick" since it was first built in 1670.

Musée Matisse trompe l'oeil windows.

In French the word "souvenir" means both "memory" and "memorabilia," capturing both the spiritual and the tangible remnants of journeys taken. It is a word that describes the collection of the Musée Matisse, which is as much a walk through Matisse's life, studios, homes, and career as it is a place to look at art. At this "biographical museum," the many pilgrims who make their way here in order to know Matisse better are well rewarded throughout the three floors and eighteen rooms of exhibitions.

The Musée Matisse owns many of Matisse's greatest works, particularly the large cutouts he made at the Régina in his final days. There are also many studies and finished paintings from the *Odalisque* series. Many of his earliest paintings are here, including student work from Bohain as well as many of the Fauve masterpieces. Those familiar with Matisse's work will recognize many of the props featured so prominently in his paintings. The Venetian Rococo chair, African carvings, small porcelain jars, and elaborate Art Nouveau vases are all on display near the paintings that made them famous. But it is the sight of so many Matisse paintings, some recognizable, some unknown, that mesmerizes even the most casual observer.

The museum's collection spans the entirety of an amazingly colorful career. Matisse's work changed and evolved over the forty years he lived in and around Nice, and the Musée Matisse reflects that remarkable evolution.

Alfred Barr Jr., the Rockefellers were able to persuade Matisse to take the commission.

After finishing the window, Matisse wrote a short note to Pierre saying that he felt in good health and was happy about this project. But later that day he suffered a small stroke. "He stopped working," his doctor wrote, "and applied himself to dying." To Lydia, the doctor whispered out of the patient's earshot, "This is the end."

When later that evening Matisse said he felt "out of sorts," Lydia said it must be his annual bout with the flu and told him to get some rest. The next afternoon, after washing her hair, Lydia came to check on Matisse, who was lying in his mobile bed, looking out the windows toward Nice. He asked her to bring him some paper and a ballpoint pen, and he began to draw.

Matisse's final work: the Rockefeller rose window at the Union Church of Pocantico Hills.

Henri Matisse died the next day, November 3, 1954, with his daughter, Marguerite, at his side. Lydia left the Hôtel Régina within the hour. Amélie arrived that night and assumed her role as the Widow Matisse, one she embraced until her own death four years later.

More than fifty years after his death, Henri Matisse is frequently recognized as one of the most important and most inspiring artists of the twentieth century. But he remains, in many ways, misunderstood. As an artist who seemed to celebrate pleasure in works that sought to capture emotion, he is most often dismissed as not serious enough.

"What I dream of is an art of balance, of purity and serenity," Matisse wrote in 1908, "devoid of troubling or depressing subject matter, an art which could be for every worker, for the business man as well as the man of letters, for example, a soothing, calming influence on the mind, something like a good armchair which provides relaxation from physical fatigue."

Matisse made four sketches of Lydia, each about six inches high, using a fresh sheet of paper each time. When he had finished, he handed her the sheets of paper and pen. Then he asked to see the last of the four drawings once again. He held it before him, not quite at arm's length. He looked it over, severely. Then he said, "It's good."

For many, the idea of art as an armchair is both simplistic and sophomoric. Indeed, Matisse's pared-down compositions often brought ridicule, his explosive Fauvist work brought condemnation, and his evocative

**Top: Eglise et Monastère Franciscain de Cimiez, circa 1900.
Left: Matisse on the balcony of his La Régina apartment.**

Odalisques brought disdain. But through it all, Matisse was never deterred. Although the criticism stung and the ignorance annoyed, he never exhausted his capacity to try, his desire to create, or his will to push forward.

"People must live," Matisse believed, "and bear their burdens with a light heart."

A Final Resting Place

After the Romans left Cimiez to fall to ruins, the Franciscan monks of nearby Genoa were the next to take up residence in the hills above Nice. From the thirteenth through the eighteenth centuries they were, in fact, the only residents.

❻ The Eglise et Monastère Franciscain de Cimiez, Avenue du Monastère de Cimiez, was built in the sixteenth century, though it was heavily restored in the 1890s as part of the campaign to make Cimiez a more enticing vacation destination. Inside are frescoes, engravings, sculptures, and altars dating back nearly a thousand years and documenting life in the monastery throughout much of that time. Surrounding the church and monastery are beautiful gardens with tropical flowers planted to create designs in the lawn, trellises of tumbling blossoms, and arbors dripping in vines.

To the south is the sea, and along the north wall is an entrance to the monastery's cemetery. For more than five hundred years, residents of Cimiez and nearby Nice have been buried here. And like so many French cemeteries, this one seems claustrophobic as a result of the mere millimeters of space between each elaborate monument. These are no simple markers. Each is a work of art, a testament not only to the deceased whom it commemorates but also to a dramatic style of the century from which it dates.

Despite many requests from officials in Vence, and even some church officials, that he choose La Chapelle du Vence as his final resting place, Matisse firmly refused on the grounds that his burial there might turn the chapel into something vain and sacrilegious. Eventually, he chose the cemetery in Cimiez instead. The city of Nice provided the land, the archbishop presided over the funeral, and the mayor delivered a eulogy. Although he had been born in the northern town of Bohain, kept a home and studio in Paris for half a century, and traveled extensively throughout Europe, Matisse came to symbolize Nice and he became an icon of the Riviera as much as the color he could never stop chasing.

The cemetery at Cimiez today.

A visitor to the cemetery can follow paths that twist and turn between and around the many crowded rows of stones. One can traverse the breadth and then the width of the hillside cemetery while encountering no sign of the artist's resting place. Then a small and shady gravel path appears, leading down the hill; another sign appears; and it becomes clear that this is the right direction.

Matisse's burial site, behind the monastery and its cemetery, is a private garden surrounded by blossoms and branches, facing the sea and drenched in sun. In the end, Matisse immersed himself in these views—the indigo blue of the water, the five hundred colors of green in the foliage, the rose glow of the sun over the mountains, and the transparent light shimmering off the sea and sky. This is where his journey ended. And when Amélie's own journey ended in 1958, the Matisse children buried their mother by his side.

Blue Nude II
(1952).

Timeline

1869 — Henri-Emile-Benoît Matisse is born in Le Cateau-Cambrésis in the Picardy region of northern France. His family moves to the nearby village of Bohain-en-Vermandois eight days later.

1887 — Matisse spends the year studying law in Paris.

1890 — Matisse is hospitalized for a hernia and tries painting for the first time.

1891 — Matisse moves to Paris to study art in October. He fails the entrance exam for the Ecole des Beaux-Arts and enrolls at Académie Julian.

1892 — Matisse is accepted as student by Gustave Moreau. He takes additional classes at the Ecole des Arts Décoratifs, fails the Beaux-Arts entrance exam for the second time, and moves to an attic apartment at 19 quai St. Michel. He begins a relationship with Caroline Joblaud (Camille).

1894 — Marguerite is born. Matisse fails the Beaux-Arts exam for the fourth time.

1895 — Matisse finally gains admission to the Ecole des Beaux-Arts and sees his first Cézanne exhibit at Vollard's gallery.

1898 — Matisse marries Amélie Noémie Alexandrine Parayre (born in 1872) in January. The couple honeymoons in London, Toulouse, and Corsica.

1899 — Matisse exhibits for the last time at the Salon de la Société Nationale des Beaux-Arts. He quits the Ecole des Beaux-Arts and moves to larger apartments at 19 quai St. Michel. Son Pierre is born.

1900 — Son Jean is born. Matisse works on Grand Palais decorations for the Exposition Universelle.

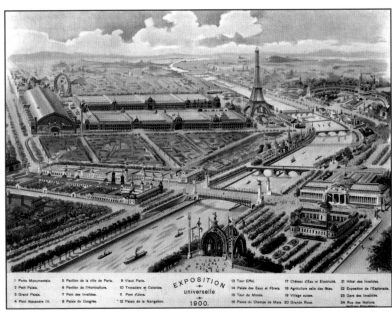

Tourist map from the 1900 Exposition Universelle.

1901 — Matisse exhibits for the first time at the Salon des Indépendants. He travels to Switzerland to recuperate from bronchitis.

1903 — Matisse exhibits at the first Salon d'Automne.

1904 — Matisse spends the summer in St. Tropez with Paul Signac and Henri Cross; he shows thirteen paintings at the annual Salon d'Automne.

1905 — Matisse exhibits *Luxe, calme et volupté* at the Salon des Indépendants. He spends the summer in Collioure with André Derain. Les Fauves debut at the Salon d'Automne.

1906 — Matisse exhibits *Bonheur de vivre* at the Salon des Indépendants. He spends the summer in Collioure and meets Pablo Picasso at the home of Gertrude Stein in the fall.

1912 — Matisse spends the winter in Morocco. He returns to Paris for the spring and summer, then returns to Morocco in the fall.

1914 — World War I starts. Matisse paintings in Berlin and Moscow are confiscated. He spends the summer in Collioure.

1918 — A joint exhibition of the work of Pablo Picasso and Henri Matisse is held at the Paul Guillaume Gallery in Paris. Matisse travels to Nice and stays at the Hôtel Beau Rivage (March and April) and the Villa des Allies (May and June). He spends several summer months in Paris before returning to Nice in September.

1921 — Matisse settles in Nice permanently and rents apartments at 1 place Charles Felix. The Musée du Luxembourg purchases *Odalisque with Red Culottes*, the first French museum purchase of a Matisse painting.

Matisse was fond of his many grandchildren, including Marguerite's son Claude, pictured here with his grandfather on the balcony of the Place Felix apartment, 1935ca.

1923 — Forty-eight Matisse paintings donated by Russian collectors form the basis of the first museum of modern art in Moscow, now known as the Pushkin Museum. Marguerite Matisse marries Georges Duthuit, art critic and scholar.

1927 — Matisse wins first prize at the International Carnegie Exhibition in Pittsburgh. Son Pierre organizes a Matisse exhibit in New York.

1930 — Matisse travels to New York, journeys to San Francisco by train, and then sets sail for Tahiti on the RMS *Tahiti*, a battered English mail boat. He returns to Nice in July, after five months of traveling.

1934 — Matisse works on illustrations for James Joyce's *Ulysses*. Lydia Delectorskaya begins working for the Matisse family.

1937 — At the Exhibition des Maîtres de l'Art Indépendant (Masters of Independent Art exhibition) held at the Petit Palais in Paris, an entire room is devoted to Matisse.

1938 — Matisse and Picasso hold joint exhibits in Copenhagen and Stockholm. Matisse travels to Switzerland and buys an apartment at the Hôtel Régina in Cimiez.

1939 — Matisse separates from Amélie. He spends several months living in the Hôtel Lutetia in Paris during divorce proceedings and estate negotiations. He paints *Music*, a companion to the mural *Dance*.

1940 — Matisse acquires a visa for a trip to Brazil, but World War II starts, so he cancels the trip and flees Paris for Nice. He begins to suffer from severe abdominal pain.

1941 — Matisse undergoes emergency surgery in Lyon for intestinal cancer in January. He suffers two heart attacks during his recovery and returns to Nice in May. He begins working with paper cutouts.

1943 — Matisse moves to Le Rêve in Vence; he works on cutouts for *Jazz*.

1946 — Matisse begins work on La Chapelle du Rosaire in Vence. The Musée National d'Art Moderne in Paris begins its Matisse collection.

1949 — The first major French museum exhibition of Matisse is held at the Musée National d'Art Moderne in Paris.

1950 — Matisse moves to the Hôtel Régina in Cimiez; he finishes work on La Chapelle.

1951 — The dedication of La Chapelle du Rosaire in Vence. A retrospective exhibit is held at the Museum of Modern Art in New York; additional exhibits are held in Cleveland, Chicago, San Francisco, and Tokyo.

Matisse continues to draw large crowds. This exhibition in 2005 featured his cutouts and many illustrations from letters to friends and family.

1952 — The Musée Matisse opens in Matisse's birthplace of Le Cateau. Matisse works exclusively on cutouts and finishes *Zulma*, *Blue Nude*, *The Sorrow of the King*, *The Negress*, and *Oceania*.

1954 — Matisse dies on November 3 at the Hôtel Régina in Cimiez.

One of Matisse's final cutouts, Tristesse du roi (The Saddness of the King), completed in 1952.

Notes

Chapter 1

3: "The search for color . . .": Matisse, quoted in "Matisse Speaks," *Art News*, November 1951, reprinted in Jack Flam, *Matisse: A Retrospective* (New York: Park Lane, 1988), 28.

6: "From the moment I held the box of colors . . .": Matisse, quoted in Hilary Spurling, *The Unknown Matisse, A Life of Henri Matisse: The Early Years, 1869–1908* (Berkeley: University of California Press, 1998), 46.

6: "There were no painters in my family . . .": Matisse, quoted in Spurling, *The Unknown Matisse*, 59.

6: "Before, nothing interested me . . .": Matisse, quoted in Spurling, *The Unknown Matisse*, 61.

7: "I was like someone who'd arrived in a country . . .": Matisse, quoted in Spurling, *The Unknown Matisse*, 68.

10: "In effect, I was going to be forced to take another profession . . .": Matisse, quoted in "A Conversation with Henri Matisse," *L'Art Vivant*, 1925, reprinted in Flam, 30.

13: "a cauldron of . . . poverty, disease . . .": Quoted in Colin Jones, *Paris: The Biography of a City* (New York: Viking, 2004), 362.

13: "Mademoiselle, I love you dearly . . .": Matisse, quoted in Spurling, *The Unknown Matisse*, 148.

15: During the model's break . . . : Matisse, in interviews with Raymond Escholier, director of the Museum of the City of Paris at the Petit Palais, recounted in Flam, 32.

15: "I know how arduous . . .": Letter from Matisse to Simon Bussy, July 1903, reprinted in Flam, 41–42.

17: In addition to the freedom . . . : From John Russell, *The World of Matisse* (New York: Time Life, 1969), 31.

18: "If I am wrong, then Cézanne is wrong . . .": Matisse, quoted in Gilles Néret, *Henri Matisse* (Glasgow: Taschen, 2002), 20.

18: "I have come to know this canvas quite well . . .": Matisse, quoted in Spurling, *The Unknown Matisse*, 182.

18: "What was taken to be boldness . . .": Matisse, quoted in Spurling, *The Unknown Matisse*, 66.

Chapter 2

22: "A strange wind . . .": Letter from Paul Signac to his mother, May 1892, quoted in Barbara Freed, *Artists and Their Museums on the Riviera* (New York: Abrams, 1998), 22–23.

22: "You talk of my going south . . .": Matisse, quoted in Spurling, *The Unknown Matisse*, 272.

23: "doomed to inevitable ruination . . .": Quoted in Henry Servat, *In the Spirit of St. Tropez: From A to Z* (Paris: Assouline, 2003), 3.

23: "St. Tropez is the capital . . .": Guy de Maupassant, Sur L'Eau (1888), quoted in Spurling, *The Unknown Matisse*, 280.

25: "Picture it on a day when . . .": Matisse, letter to Henri Manguin, 1904, reprinted in Flam, 46.

27: The twenty-year love affair . . .: Quotations in the paragraph are from Freed, 22–23.

30: "In the cool of the morning . . .": Matisse, letter to Manguin, 1904.

31: "The sheen of sun oil . . .": Quoted in Servat, 148.

32: "Since I got here . . .": Matisse, letter to Manguin, 1904.

33: "I know well that the question of money for survival . . .": Henri Cross, letter to Matisse, quoted in Spurling, *The Unknown Matisse,* 286.

35: "If you want to properly draw mountains . . .": Cennino Cennini, quoted in Xavier Girad, *Mediterranean: From Homer to Picasso* (New York: Assouline, 2001), 37.

36: "gone completely to the dogs . . .": Signac, letter to Charles Angrand, January 14, 1906, quoted in Spurling, *The Unknown Matisse,* 337.

37: "those who will not be content . . ." and "The triumphant colorist . . .": Signac, *From Delacroix to Pointilism,* quoted in John Russell, *The World of Matisse* (New York: Time Life, 1969), 38.

37: "It is good but you will not remain with it . . .": Henri Cross to Matisse, quoted in Néret, 25.

37: "One cannot live in a household that is too well-kept. . .": Matisse, quoted in Néret, 26.

Chapter 3

40: "It is this intense light, this perpetual dazzlement . . .": Paul Soulier, quoted in Spurling, *The Unknown Matisse,* 299.

47: Les Templiers sidebar: From James Morgan, *Chasing Matisse: A Year in France Living My Dream* (New York:

Free Press, 2005), chapter 7.

49: "Is this still France . . .": Quoted in Spurling, *The Unknown Matisse,* 299.

52: "From the moment I saw my first Matisse . . .": Pablo Picasso, quoted in Dan Franck, *Bohemian Paris: Picasso, Modigliani, Matisse, and the Birth of Modern Art* (New York: Grove Press, 2001), 102.

52: "Matisse is color; Picasso is form . . .": Wassily Kandinsky, quoted in Néret, 42.

52: "We must talk to each other . . .": Matisse to Picasso, quoted in Flam, 373.

53: "That's not painting": Anna Matisse, quoted in Spurling, *The Unknown Matisse,* 330.

54: Derivation of the term "fauve" is from Flam, 46–47.

54: "We belong to our time . . .": Matisse, quoted in Flam, 46–47.

Chapter 4

58: "I was just emerging from long and tiring years . . .": Matisse, quoted in Néret, 99.

58: "As for telling you what it will be like . . .": Letter from Matisse to his wife, quoted in Jack Cowart, *Henri Matisse: The Early Years in Nice* (New York: Abrams, 1986), 19.

61: "I can scarce help thinking myself enchanted . . .": Tobias Smollett, quoted in Robert Kanigel, *High Season: How One French Riviera Town Has Seduced Travelers for Two Thousand Years* (New York: Viking, 2002), 19.

63: "Strolling there last Christmas . . .": Arthur Young, quoted in Kanigel, 52.

63: "Most people come here . . .": Matisse, quoted in Cowart, 19.

64: "I'm from the North . . .": Matisse, quoted in Néret, 105.

64: "I feel like a human being again": Matisse, letter to Amélie, May 16, 1918, quoted in Hilary Spurling, *Matisse the Master, A Life of Henri Matisse: The Conquest of Colour, 1909–1954* (New York: Alfred A. Knopf, 2005), 210.

66: "I'm the hermit . . .": Matisse, letter to his wife, quoted in Cowart, 29.

65: "His life was a long martyrdom . . .": Matisse, quoted in Cowart, 19.

68: His new home in Nice . . . : From Russell, *The World of Matisse*, 122.

70: "Everything is fake, absurd, amazing, delicious": Matisse, quoted in Jean-Bernard Naudin, *Matisse: A Way of Life in the South of France* (New York: Rizzoli, 1997), 28.

71: "Matisse is a name that rhymes with Nice . . .": Pierre Schneider, quoted in Néret, 7.

74: "There is only one thing that counts in the long run . . .": Matisse, quoted in Flam, 379.

Chapter 5

81: "Those were years so stabbingly felt . . .": Donald Culross Peattie, *Immortal Village* (Chicago: University of Chicago Press, 1945), xiii.

83: Matisse's Women and the War sidebar: From John Russell, *Matisse: Father and Son* (New York: Abrams, 1999), 237–38.

85: "I told my surgeons in Lyon that I needed three years of good health . . .": Matisse, quoted in Spurling, *Matisse the Master*, 428.

88: "I'm not saying that I can bring them perfection . . .": Matisse, letter to his son Pierre, quoted in Russell, *Matisse: Father and Son*, 363.

88: "The interest he had found in studying, in musing . . .": Matisse, quoted in Freed, 169.

89: Letter to the bishop, reprinted in Freed, 168.

90: "In summary . . .": Matisse, *L'Illustration*, Christmas 1951, quoted in *Chapelle du Rosaire of the Dominican Nuns of Vence by Henri Matisse*, available at the chapel in Vence.

91: A Question of Faith sidebar: From Flam, 371.

95: "He has lived through . . .": Alfred Frankfurter, quoted in Flam, 351.

Chapter 6

99: "This land of Roman gods . . .": Smollett, quoted in Kanigel, 23.

100: "I do not want to say . . .": J. C. Harris, quoted in Kanigel, 128.

102: "marvelous, on the one side . . .": Queen Victoria, quoted in Kanigel, 131.

103: "I am beginning to take Renoir's place . . .": Matisse, quoted in Spurling, *Matisse the Master*, 465.

104: "the models' ballet": Hélène Adant, photographer and friend of Lydia's, quoted in Marie-France Boyer, *Matisse at Villa le Rêve* (London: Thames and Hudson, 2004), 57.

105: "I think that it has an exceptional quality . . .": Matisse, letter to his son Pierre, quoted in Russell, *Matisse: Father and Son*, 363.

106: "A scattering of color . . .": Quoted in Spurling, *Matisse the Master*, 463–65.

107: "What counts for me . . .": Matisse, quoted in
Russell, *Matisse: Father and Son*, 365.

108: "Don't move! . . .": Lydia Delectorskaya, quoted in
Spurling, *Matisse the Master*, 355.

108: "I never expected . . .": Sister Jacques-Marie
(Monique Bourgeois), quoted in Russell, *Matisse: Father
and Son*, 376.

110: After finishing the window . . . : Lydia recounted
these events in the epilogue to her book, *Contre Vents
et Marées* (1939). Her account of Matisse's death is
quoted in Russell, *Matisse: Father and Son*, 377, and
Spurling, *Matisse the Master*, 466.

110: "What I dream of is an art of balance . . .":
Matisse, "Notes of a Painter, December 25, 1908,"
reprinted in Flam, 76.

111: "People must live . . .": Matisse, interview by
Marie Raymond, 1953, reprinted in Flam, 384.

For Further Reading

Boyer, Marie-France. *Matisse at Villa le Rêve*. London: Thames and Hudson, 2004.

Cowart, Jack, and Dominique Fourcade. *Henri Matisse: The Early Years in Nice, 1916–1930*. New York: Abrams, 1986.

Flam, Jack. *Matisse: A Retrospective*. New York: Park Lane, 1988.

Franck, Dan. *Bohemian Paris: Picasso, Modigliani, Matisse, and the Birth of Modern Art*. Trans. Cynthia Hope Liebow. New York: Grove Press, 2001.

Kanigel, Robert. *High Season: How One French Riviera Town Has Seduced Travelers for Two Thousand Years*. New York: Viking, 2002.

Lassaigne, Jacques. *Matisse: Biographical and Critical Study*. Trans. Stuart Gilbert. Paris: Skira, 1959.

Matamoros, Joséphine, and Dominique Szymusiak. *Matisse et Derain: 1905, un été à Collioure*. Paris: Gallimard, 2005.

Millet, Laurence. *The Little Book of Matisse*. Paris: Flammarion, 2002.

Naudin, Jean-Bernard. *Matisse: A Way of Life in the South of France*. New York: Rizzoli, 1997.

Néret, Gilles. *Henri Matisse*. Glasgow: Taschen, 2002.

Peattie, Donald Culross. *Immortal Village*. Chicago: University of Chicago Press, 1945.

Russell, John. *Matisse: Father and Son*. New York: Abrams, 1999.

———. *The World of Matisse*. New York: Time Life, 1969.

Spurling, Hilary. *Matisse the Master, A Life of Henri Matisse: The Conquest of Colour, 1909–1954*. New York: Alfred A. Knopf, 2005.

———. *The Unknown Matisse, A Life of Henri Matisse: The Early Years, 1869–1908*. Berkeley: University of California Press, 1998.

Index

Credits

Image on page 21 © 2006 Artists Rights Society (ARS), New York / ADAGP, Paris.

Image on page 36, *The Joy of Life*, 1905-06 (oil on canvas), and image on page 64, *Blue Villa, Nice*, 1917 (oil on panel), © The Barnes Foundation, Merion, Pennsylvania, USA, © Succession H. Matisse / DACS / The Bridgeman Art Library.

Image on page 91, photograph by Robert Capa, copyright © 2001 by Cornell Capa/Magnum Photos.

Images on pages 20 and 38 from Dreamstime.

Image on page 55 Giraudon / Art Resource NY.

Image on page 110 courtesy of Historic Hudson Valley, Tarrytown, N.Y., www.hudsonvalley.org.

Image on page 34, *The Terrace, St. Tropez,* 1904 (oil on canvas), © Isabella Stewart Gardner Museum, Boston, MA, USA, © Succession H. Matisse / DACS / The Bridgeman Art Library.

Image on page 56 from Istockphoto.com.

Image on page 96 courtesy of Robert Kanigel.

Image on page 54 copyright Jacqueline Marval.

Images on pages 3, 5, 8 (photo of Matisse and students), 10, 11 (both images), 13 (both images), 18, 28 (*The Gate to Signac's Studio*), 32, 33 (*Woman with an Umbrella*), 44, 45 (both images), 48 (*Closed Window at Collioure*), 65 (Matisse with Renoir), 69, 71, 72, 73, 74, 78, 85 (both images), 86 (both images), 103, 105, 106, 108, 113, 116, and 117 (*The Sadness of the King*) © Succession H. Matisse.

Images on pages 95, 107, and 111 (Matisse on the balcony) The Pierre Matisse Gallery Archives, The Pierpont Morgan Library, New York, MA 5020. Photo credit: The Pierpont Morgan Library / Art Resource, NY.

Digital image on page 63 © The Museum of Modern Art / Licensed by SCALA / Art Resource, NY.

Image on page 48, *Open Window, Collioure*, collection of Mr. and Mrs. John Hay Whitney, image © 2006 Board of Trustees, National Gallery of Art.

Image on page 101 (postcard) courtesy Michael Nelson, from *Queen Victoria and the Discovery of the Riviera* (I. B. Tauris, 2001).

Image on page 60 courtesy Nice Convention & Visitors Bureau.

Image on page 2 courtesy Charles Penny.

Image on page 17 courtesy Photothèque des Musées de la Ville de Paris.

Image in page 76 from http://www.provencebeyond.

Images on pages 8 (*Hesiod and the Muse*), 49, 84, 88, 90, 92, and 93 (*The Stations of the Cross*) Réunion des Musées Nationaux / Art Resource, NY. Image on page 31 © Willy Rizzo Galerie Agathe Gaillard.

Image on page 9 from roi-president.com, by Frederic Valdes and Malissin Pierre-Emmanuel.

Image on page 53, *Femme au chapeau* (Woman in a Hat), 1905; oil on canvas; 31 3/4 in. x 23 1/2 in. (80.65 cm x 59.69 cm); San Francisco Museum of Modern Art; Bequest of Elise S. Haas; © Succession H. Matisse, Paris / Artists Rights Society (ARS), New York.

Image on page 35 Scala / Art Resource, NY.

Images on pages 65 (Les Collettes) and 83 courtesy Michael Swanson.

Image on page 14 (*Notre Dame*), Tate Gallery, London / Art Resource, NY.

Image on page 50 (wine bottle) courtesy Sami and Emma Toutonji.

Image on page 52 is from the U.S. Library of Congress, Prints & Photographs Division, [LC-USZ62-98505].

Image on page 104 (Katherine Dunham) is from the U.S. Library of Congress, Prints & Photographs Division [LC-USZ62-123620].

All other images are in the author's or publisher's collection or in the public domain.

About the Author

Laura McPhee works and lives in Indianapolis, Indiana. She received her BA in French and English from Indiana University in 1998 and her MA in English from Indiana University in 2003. As both an undergraduate and a graduate student, she spent multiple semesters studying in France at the American University in Paris and the University of Burgundy in Dijon. Currently, she is a contributing editor at *NUVO*, the alternative newsweekly in Indianapolis, where she covers politics and social justice issues. In 2006, she received multiple awards for her news and feature writing, including four awards from the Society of Professional Journalists.

About the ArtPlace Series

This book is part of the ArtPlace series published by Roaring Forties Press. Each book in the series explores how a renowned artist and a world-famous city or area helped to define and inspire each other. ArtPlace volumes are intended to stimulate both eye and mind, offering a rich mix of art and photography, history and biography, ideas and information. While the books can be used by tourists to navigate and illuminate their way through cityscapes and landscapes, the volumes can also be read by armchair travelers in search of an engrossing and revealing story.

Other titles include *A Journey into Dorothy Parker's New York, A Journey into Steinbeck's California, A Journey into the Transcendentalists' New England, A Journey into Georgia O'Keeffe's New Mexico, A Journey into Ireland's Literary Revival,* and *A Journey into Flaubert's Normandy.*

Visit Roaring Forties Press's website, www.roaringfortiespress.com, for details of these and other forthcoming titles, as well as to learn about upcoming author tours, media appearances, and all kinds of special events and offers. Visitors to the website may also send comments and questions to the authors of the ArtPlace series books.

A Journey into Matisse's South of France

This book is set in Goudy and Futura; the display type is Futura Condensed. The cover and the interior were designed by Jeff Urbancic. Sherri Schultz and Deirdre Greene edited the text, which was proofread by Desne Ahlers and indexed by Sonsie Conroy.